BIEDERMANN UND DIE BRANDSTIFTER

TWENTIETH CENTURY GERMAN TEXTS

ANSICHTEN EINES CLOWNS by Heinrich Böll
Edited by William Hanson

DER AUFHALTSAME AUFSTIEG DES ARTURO UI by Bertolt Brecht
Edited by D.G. and S.M. Matthews

DER GUTE MENSCH VON SEZUAN by Bertolt Brecht
Edited by Bruce Thompson

DER KAUKASISCHE KREIDEKREIS by Bertolt Brecht
Edited by Bruce Thompson

FÜNF LEHRSTÜCKE by Bertolt Brecht
Edited by Keith A. Dickson

DER BESUCH DER ALTEN DAME by Friedrich Dürrenmatt
Edited by Paul Ackermann

ANDORRA by Max Frisch
Edited by H.F. Garten

BIEDERMANN UND DIE BRANDSTIFTER by Max Frisch
Edited by Peter Hutchinson

DON JUAN ODER DIE LIEBE ZUR GEOMETRIE by Max Frisch
Edited by D.G. and S.M. Matthews

DER JÜNGSTE TAG by Ödön von Horváth
Edited by Ian Huish

DIE VERWANDLUNG by Franz Kafka
Edited by Peter Hutchinson and Michael Minden

IM WESTEN NICHTS NEUES by Erich Maria Remarque
Edited by Brian Murdoch

DER HAUPTMANN VON KÖPENICK by Carl Zuckmayer
Edited by H.F. Garten

SCHACHNOVELLE by Stefan Zweig
Edited by Brian Murdoch

TWENTIETH CENTURY TEXTS

Max Frisch

BIEDERMANN UND DIE BRANDSTIFTER

Ein Lehrstück ohne Lehre

Edited by
Peter Hutchinson

Lecturer in German,
University of Cambridge
Fellow and Director of Studies
in Modern Languages,
Trinity Hall

First published in 1986 by
Methuen & Co. Ltd

Reprinted 1988, 1989, 1990
by Routledge
11 New Fetter Lane, London EC4P 4EE

Printed in Great Britain by
Richard Clay, Ltd,
Bungay, Suffolk.

British Library Cataloguing in Publication Data

Frisch, Max
[Herr Biedermann und die Brandstifter]
Biedermann und die Brandstifter:
ein Lehrstück ohne Lehre. –
(Twentieth century texts)
I. [Herr Biedermann und die Brandstifter]
II. Title III. Hutchinson, Peter 1944–
832'.912 PT2611.R814

ISBN 0-415-02758-6

CONTENTS

ACKNOWLEDGEMENT

The editor and publishers are grateful to Suhrkamp Verlag for permission to reproduce the text in this edition.

PREFACE

A text which will be used extensively in British sixth forms should not, perhaps, be edited by one whose acquaintance with sixth-form difficulties is now out of date. The preparation of the notes and select vocabulary has therefore been determined on the advice of a number of sixth-formers (from a variety of schools) who were prepared to read the play and honestly indicate their difficulties. In this connection I should like to thank Fiona Cushley, Warren Gray, Charles Hagon, and Jonathan Proctor. I should also like to acknowledge the help of Mr Alan Cutts of Farnborough (Sixth Form) College, and Mr Michael Oswald of Newcastle upon Tyne Royal Grammar School. Further assistance was freely given by my colleague Lisa Llewellyn and my pupil Nev Tewfik, and I am grateful to my former pupil Ian Sanderson for help with the proofs.

Peter Hutchinson
Trinity Hall, Cambridge

INTRODUCTION

MAX FRISCH: LIFE AND WORKS

Knowledge of the circumstances in which an author matured and wrote his works may place us in a better position to appreciate his techniques and his themes. In the case of Franz Kafka, for example, critics never tire of explaining how parents, religion, social background, and a curious linguistic position played a crucial role in determining a strange choice of subject-matter and an unprecedented handling of it. Indeed, some critics claim that we cannot even begin to understand Kafka's work without a sound acquaintance with his life and times. With Frisch, however, the case is less convincing. Knowledge of his life may be of interest to us, yet it is by no means essential to our appreciation of *Biedermann*, a play which transcends the period and circumstances in which it was written.

Frisch was born in Zurich in 1911. He began writing plays at the age of 16, and on leaving school he spent two years at Zurich University studying German literature. After the death of his father he did not have the financial support to continue, and so for the three following years he travelled widely in south-east Europe as a free-lance reporter. During this period he wrote his first novel, but the need to find a more secure form of existence led him to enrol as a student of architecture at the Technical University in Zurich. (His father had been an architect, and the young Frisch was now supported by the generosity of a wealthy friend.) He graduated in 1941 and in 1942 won a prize for his first major architectural project. He established his own small firm, and until 1950, when he devoted himself almost completely to writing, he effectively practised two professions.

Although Frisch began to write early in his life, he burnt all his manuscripts in 1937 and vowed never to write again. The beginnings of war in Europe changed his mind, and his call-up in 1939 is reflected in 'Blätter aus dem Brotsack' of 1940. Switzerland remained neutral throughout the war, but Frisch was obliged to remain a reservist after his basic period of service. Despite his duties here and his architectural tasks too, he nevertheless managed to publish a well-received novel in 1943, and then, in 1945, his first play to be staged. From this point on he produced a succession of plays and novels (many of these becoming bestsellers); he also wrote a number of essays and published his diaries. *Biedermann* was first produced in 1958, when the author's reputation was rising sharply (after the two successful novels *Stiller* and *Homo Faber*), and its success contributed probably more than any other work to his international popularity. Since then he has written much fiction, drama, and polemical pieces, he has continued to travel widely, and he has received a large number of literary prizes.

Frisch's concerns have not changed much over five decades. Even in his earliest writings many of the basic ideas of his maturity are readily evident. He is a largely conservative writer (both in content and technique) and he is often concerned with intellectuals, their sense of identity, and their problems of communication with others. Other issues which appear regularly in his works include Man's need to understand himself, the importance of moral responsibility, and the individual's entrapment in a certain social role. The meaning of life and of love, and the search for happiness are also recurrent themes. There is regular criticism of contemporary society, as well as unease over the status and the materialism of his own country. Frisch expects his works to encourage readers and audiences to question themselves, and especially their motivation. He achieves this in a directly challenging way, enabling them to see aspects of their own position in his central figures and their problems.

THE DEVELOPMENT OF BIEDERMANN

The core of the play is contained in a six-page sketch in Frisch's *Tagebuch* for 1948. A man, who claims he has suffered injustice, is given shelter by a sympathetic listener partly because the listener feels sorry for the man, and partly because he fears being the victim of the revenge which the man claims will one day be his due. The visitor is offered a bed for the night, but he prefers the loft. The host becomes uneasy, recalling recent stories of arson, but he dismisses these by reminding himself that more trust in humanity is needed. Nevertheless, his unease prevails as the guest continues to inhabit the loft and actually introduces a friend who, he openly admits, has been imprisoned for arson. The host regains his peace of mind by re-reading an (unnamed) morality play by Max Mell [*Das Apostelspiel*, in which two villains do not carry out their murderous intent because one of them is so humbled by the innocent Christian belief of the daughter of their host], but he is later shaken to discover barrels of petrol are being taken into his loft. The visitors' frankness about this is almost as disconcerting as it is reassuring – surely true arsonists would never admit to such a thing! Equally, their jokes about looking for wood shavings, wanting to set the whole town ablaze, and waiting for the right wind cannot be serious: true arsonists would, of course, act differently. Yet it is with an increasing conflict of the emotions of fear, desire for peace and quiet, and the selfish thought that befriending the men could mean self-preservation, that the host invites his guests for an evening bottle of wine. As they leave, they ask for matches, and by the next day the host and his belongings have gone up in smoke.

48 Burleske

The tone of this sketch, which Frisch entitled 'Burleske' ('farce') is light-hearted and intimate. The imagined host is in fact the reader (who is cosily addressed as 'du') and he is attributed with a number of bourgeois features: mild sympathy, desire for peace and quiet, desire to appear generous, half-hearted notions of belief in the goodness of one's fellow man; but he is also attributed with indecision, selfish fears, and culpable gullibility. The humour derives from the ironic presentation, the way in which the narrator largely identifies himself with the host's position, gaily explaining away awkward facts but maintaining just sufficient distance to warn his reader that disaster is *almost* certain to follow.

Late in 1949 Frisch produced an eight-page outline for a radio play on the same subject; he was obviously dissatisfied with it, for it was not until 1952 that he properly set to work on the text. His reasons for the choice of the material were not fascination with its themes: the motivation was partly financial (he needed the money) and partly practical (he could think of nothing else). Although he had never written a radio play before (and, he claimed, never even heard one), the product is quite slick; it is, however, by no means as subtle as the ensuing play for the stage.

49 Hörspiel

There are two major differences between 'Burleske' and 'Hörspiel'. Most importantly, the figure of 'Biedermann' makes his first appearance. His guilty conscience (to which only vague reference is made in the 'farce') is made specific (his part in the suicide of Knechtling), and he is most concerned not to be seen as a 'philistine' ('Spießer'). Second, the listeners know from the start what has happened. A commentator, who is actually labelled 'Verfasser', informs us in advance of the disaster, telling us that Biedermann himself handed over the matches; with tongue in cheek he denies Biedermann's culpability, and throughout the play he questions the listeners on whether they would have acted any differently. In this version the town is actually given a fairy-tale name, *Seldwyla* (the name of an imaginary place in the writings of the nineteenth-century Swiss novelist Gottfried

Keller, who views this creation in the first instance as a place of amusing philistines). A great number of other small features are introduced (as the material is expanded from six pages to the forty-six of a sixty-minute broadcast), many of which serve to heighten the aspects of comedy.

Despite the success of the radio play, it was not until 1957 that Frisch again returned to the material. Once more, it was financial pressures and the suggestion of the 'Schauspielhaus' Zurich that he develop the piece for the stage which prompted his decision: not the appeal of the material. The product of his two months' restructuring was first performed in early 1958 and is the version printed in this volume. It reveals a number of changes from the 'Hörspiel', the most important structural one being the introduction of the 'Chorus', which in some respects takes over the role of the 'Verfasser'. Other changes which affect our interpretation include: suppression of advance information that the house/town will be razed by fire; omission of references to *Seldwyla*; absence of any clear motivation for the arsonists; introduction of the policeman and the 'intellectual'; introduction of the 'Jedermann' scene; a more negative presentation of Biedermann and his wife.

57/8

Frisch was surprised at the success of *Biedermann*, and this may be partly due to the fact that he did not take its composition as seriously as that of his other works – his novels, for example, or the later play *Andorra*. He once referred to it as a 'five-finger exercise' to fill in time between other creations, and yet it may be precisely this lack of full engagement which has benefited the piece as far as box-office reception is concerned. There is no intensity of theme, for example, no rigorous investigation of motivation. The very different ways in which the work has been interpreted in different societies show that interpretation is left to the spectator – the dramatist does not force a view on us. We do not really see any of the urgent problems Frisch develops elsewhere with the exception, perhaps, of personal guilt – and yet this is handled ambiguously. In all three versions the point is made that in some ways you can't lay full blame on the indecisive bourgeois.

As Biedermann, stepping out of his role, puts it to the audience:

> aber Hand aufs Herz, meine Herren: Was hätten Sie denn getan, Herrgottnochmal, an meiner Stelle? Und wann?

Similarly, the ambiguous sub-title certainly reflects the views of many who leave a performance: what *is* the 'Lehre' which that provocative formulation encourages us to seek? ('Ruthlessly turn away every beggar'?) This 'uncommitted' approach to theme may have left the author in a freer position to develop the sources of spectacle and comedy to which the play principally owes its success.

LEVELS OF INTERPRETATION

Frisch almost completely avoids any sort of reference which would restrict his play to a particular country or a particular age.[1] The work has therefore been interpreted in very different ways in different parts of the world. Countries in the Eastern bloc, for example, have seen the fire-raisers as National Socialists, and in particular as Adolf Hitler in 1933. They have also emphasised that the play has relevance to developments in the Federal Republic today. Western critics have reacted differently. True, a good number of them have pointed out those levels highlighted in the East, but they have emphasized above all the relevance of the work to the Communists' rise to power in Czechoslovakia in 1948, and to methods of communist infiltration in general ('die klassische Satire gegen den Kommunismus').[2]

The Communist 'takeover' in Prague in February 1948 undoubtedly gave the spark to Frisch's first sketch. He had visited the city in January of that year, and he took a keen interest in the political developments, hoping that a socialist democracy would firmly establish itself there. In his *Tagebuch*, in fact, *immediately preceding the 'Burleske'*, is an entry on 'Umsturz in der Tschechoslowakei'.[3] Frisch notes the suddenness of events, expresses concern for his friends, and then notes the conceited response of the Swiss that such things would never be possible in their country: 'Dazu der allgemeine Dünkel: Das wäre bei uns halt nicht möglich'. The 'Burleske' could be taken as a demonstration of the folly of such an attitude.

Czechoslovakia may have served as a spark, but it provided only a partial model. The country had its first post-war elections in 1946, when the Communist Party held the greatest number of seats. Their leader, Klement Gottwald, resisted a coalition with the Social Democrats (which would have produced a majority) and pursued a policy of rebuilding the country by using figures from all the parties in what was called a 'National Front'. In the following year, however, the Communists attempted to incorporate the Social Democrats, failed to do so, and therefore began to infiltrate the police by appointment of their own members (the 'Home Secretary' was a Communist). Twelve cabinet ministers resigned in protest, thus placing the President, Beneš, in a quandary. Against a background of agitation by the Communists, the threat of a general strike, the possibility of a form of civil war, and the chance of intervention by Soviet troops, Beneš agreed to Gottwald's forming a new government of which half the members would be Communist. Several months later the Communists had taken over completely, and Gottwald himself was elected President. The Communist Party – and Gottwald in particular – had never made any secret of their desire to have complete power, and Beneš' actions are sometimes seen as a bad mistake. He complied for a mixture of motives, however: the desire to retain some control, to avoid bloodshed, to prevent Soviet forces from intervening. By that stage of the crisis he had little choice.

Any parallel between Czechoslovakia and *Biedermann* lies in situation and not in personalities. The common factor is the 'takeover' by shrewd individuals who do not disguise their real intentions. The surrounding circumstances, though, are quite different, and if Frisch had not published his diary, critics would have been far more hesitant in equating those situations. The capitalist swindler Biedermann is totally unlike the elder statesman Beneš; the anarchistic fire-raisers completely lack the ideological commitment of Gottwald. The same applies to the other historical parallel of which critics are so fond: the 'seizure' of power by the German National Socialists in 1933. As far as the personalities are concerned, Biedermann has very little in common with Hindenburg, and Schmitz/Eisenring just as little in common with Hitler. But as for policies, then it is true that Hitler did not conceal his aims and that he managed to 'dupe' Hindenburg into 'handing over' power. The linking factor here is the surrender of that power, which Frisch presents symbolically as an innocent box of matches. Fire is a simple but universal symbol of potential disaster, and these matches have maintained their suggestive power beyond any historical points of reference. As one critic has so neatly put it, 'Die Streichhölzchen wechseln mit den Zeiten'.[4] Fresh parallels will doubtless present themselves in due course.

Other symbols in the play have prompted different interpretations. The petrol drums, for example, and the figure of the 'intellectual'. The former have been seen as weapons, in particular highly destructive nuclear bombs, and their appearance in the attic has been linked with the threat of nuclear weapons appearing on West German soil in the 1950s. More recently they have been compared with intercontinental missiles introduced to Europe by the USA. The 'Dr. phil.' has also been seen in different ways: as an extremist intellectual of the left – *or of the right* – who is prepared to give totalitarianism a philosophical basis. His collaboration with the anarchists has been compared to Biedermann's:

both figures reveal that compromise with evil in fact amounts to capitulation to evil. Yet whatever suggestions of political significance may be drawn from the play, there are numerous features which prevent it from fitting neatly into any single allegory which might be proposed. In this respect the stage play shows a marked development over the radio version, and this has greatly assisted the work's international success.

Frisch has created a play of suggestions and implications, and he has left it to individuals to speculate on those which fit their own situations best.

THE CHORUS

The original Greek 'Chorus' consisted of a group of men who performed songs and dances at religious festivals; as Greek theatre evolved, they became an essential part of it, and in the earliest phase their role may have been more important than that of the actors. Indeed, the earliest forms of 'drama' probably consisted of verse exchanges between the Chorus and a single actor. As further actors were added, the Chorus retained its role as a 'participant', and its leader would step in to interrupt the action. As the actors took over the foreground, though, the Chorus became more restricted, functioning rather as occasional commentator on the action and representing the views of the audience or of the author himself.

Any age which prefers realism in drama must obviously reject the inclusion of a Chorus: the constant presence on stage, or the sudden intrusion, of a group of 'non-actors' must break any illusion of reality which has been created and remind the spectator that he is sitting in a theatre. The nineteenth century therefore, with its urgent concern for realism, had no place for such illusion-breaking features. In the early twentieth century, however, when there was an attempt to break away from the exact reproduction of social milieu, the presence of a Chorus - or of something akin to it - again began to appear acceptable. The change in attitude to the theatre of illusion was gradual, but the most decisive influence on attitudes was effected by Bertolt Brecht - his particular influence on Frisch is discussed below.

Frisch introduces his Chorus at much the same points of the action as did the later Greek dramatists, but he does not employ it for exactly the same purposes. His Chorus is in the background throughout, briefly taking the foreground at the beginning, at the end, and at the close of each scene, and at one point it actually participates in the action. Like its Greek predecessors, its function is to comment on the activities of the actors, and it urges the spectators to draw a moral. But Frisch's Chorus differs from the Greek one in several critical respects. A modern dramatist cannot expect his audience to accept a technique which is associated primarily with plays written thousands of years ago. This would represent a rather naïve anachronism. Frisch therefore makes fun of the classical Chorus, while nevertheless providing it with lines whose truth we cannot help but recognize. At the same time, his spectators have some difficulty in taking the pronouncements of the Chorus seriously, largely because it lacks the dignity of its classical forerunner. It is composed, after all, of firemen (figures of immense amusement in France and parts of Switzerland), they *chant* their lines (which would seem more appropriate to a play written entirely in verse) in a comically non-realistic manner, their leader's first remark is decidedly cynical (we do our job because we're *paid* to do it), and that leader is occasionally seen filling his pipe, not what we expect from the Chief Fireman! The language and syntax of their speech is also clearly parodistic: the rising and falling rhythms are created by constant inversion, repetition, and a highly cumbrous syntax which attempts to throw into relief certain key words; there are also unusual compound nouns and adjectives, which would again seem more appropriate in a German classical drama than in one written after 1945. Interspersed between these are jarring modern and colloquial words, as well as references to such modern concepts as petrol and the telephone. The spectator is thus thoroughly disoriented by the anachronisms, the bombast, the bathos, the trivialities, and yet the occasional *aptness* of the Chorus' message.

Frisch has denied that his intentions with the Chorus were parodistic,[5] but this is hard to accept. 'Parody' is after all, the humorous exaggeration of those features which characterize any original model, and that is precisely what Frisch manages to achieve. Furthermore, it is obvious that certain parts of the Chorus' speech are modelled on a specific classical text: the opening speech of the Second Act of Sophocles' *Antigone* as translated by Friedrich Hölderlin.[6] It could, however, be argued that Frisch occasionally goes beyond the bounds of parody and indulges in what is called 'travesty' – through wilder exaggeration and decisive breaks with certain aspects of the original, he produces moments of sheer ridiculousness. The gulf between the original model and the present text is here extreme, and not all audiences will be amused by this – not least because such moments also reveal a crude gap between a stylized fantasy world and the colloquial and far more realistic stylistic plane on which the main plot itself depends.

Frisch may be adopting certain Greek practices and actually parodying a speech from one of the most famous of all Greek plays, but there is one aspect of ancient thought which he vigorously rejects: that of fate ('Schicksal'), of what cannot be avoided ('Unabwendbares'). The Chorus denounces the popular use of this concept and urges that we reconsider events which have been 'explained away' in terms of it. Human stupidity is rather the cause, and one of the main arguments of the Chorus is that we *can* change the course of events by thinking and acting. The play actually ends with the Chorus repeating this lesson, although it also expresses doubts about whether anything can be in fact learnt.

BIEDERMANN – A COMEDY?

Classification of this play is not easy. It has at various points been claimed as 'political theatre', 'theatre of the absurd', a 'parable', and, somewhat reluctantly, a 'comedy'. Whenever the latter term has been used, it has often been combined with adjectives like 'black', 'macabre', or 'grotesque'.

Frisch has a moral purpose in *Biedermannn* – repeated unambiguously in the intrusions of the Chorus – and this is one of the factors which gives the work a more disturbing note than we would traditionally expect in the comic mode. (Comedies often have moral *implications*, but rarely an overt moral *aim*.) Furthermore, the final scene does not conclude with the traditional 'comic resolution', but with a total catastrophe, and the implications of practically every preceding scene have been pessimistic and cynical. But the humour is above all 'black' in the sense that the principal subject of the play – the anarchists' destruction of bourgeois society through easily duping its representative – bears a troubling relation to our own world. Even though we cannot identify with Biedermann, that unscrupulous business fraud, we can recognize certain all too common features of human behaviour in his actions. So although we may laugh at his repeated discomfiture (and we can do so because there is no real *emotional* bond between him and ourselves), we do also recognize the 'everyman' elements in his mentality. This troubling edge to much of the play's humour is clearly part of its 'grotesque' element.

The grotesque is a curious literary form, which derives its effects partly from exaggeration, and partly from the mixture of comic and disturbing emotions which it provokes. The spectator is aroused into an uneasy sensation in which he feels uncertain whether fear, pity, or revulsion would be more appropriate a reaction than simply laughter. In *Biedermann*, for example, we may not be able to help ourselves laughing at Schmitz's portrayal of the ghost of Knechtling. The hysterical reaction of the silly Babette (who thinks it really is a ghost), the apparently innocent defence of his choice by Schmitz, and the affected indignation of Eisenring, who makes matters worse for the Biedermanns by giving a graphic description of what Knechtling probably looks like immediately after burial, all this follows a scene of rising tension (Who is Schmitz portraying?/Will he really operate in a way similar to Hofmannsthal's 'Tod'/How will Biedermann react?), and our taut senses *need* to be relaxed through laughter. There is, in other words, a simple *physiological* necessity for our emotions to release themselves at the smallest opportunity. Yet, as we laugh, it is difficult to banish from our minds the Knechtling sub-plot, the callousness of Biedermann, the pathetic suicide, the sad position of the widow and children. Such thoughts render our laughter uneasy, possibly 'guilty'. A joke has been made out of something basically pathetic. Similarly, we may not be able to laugh wholeheartedly at the fire-raisers' remarks about organizing a preliminary diversion on the outskirts of the town (so that destruction at the centre cannot be prevented), for their techniques reveal a cruel attitude towards life and property. So too our laughter at the ludicrous attempt by the Dr. phil. to 'distance' himself may well be dampened by the implications of the horrific sounds which drown his speech. No two spectators are likely to react in exactly the same way to such moments, for we all have a different threshold for the grotesque. In addition, the interpretation adopted by the stage director can radically change our views.

Many critics consider there is a potentially sad basis to all laughter, but in much of *Biedermann* any 'troubling' roots of the comedy are too far removed from the surface to influence our reactions. Further, Frisch is often content to build his humorous dimension out of standard devices. Out of inconsistency, for example, which provides the steadiest undercurrent of humour in the play through the central character himself. In this figure we have a man who is prepared to tolerate, condone, and finally even encourage the sort of person whom he had vehemently denounced in his opening lines ('Aufhängen sollte man sie.'). His journey to such a position is the result of failure to stick to principles, self-delusion, and desperate attempts to ingratiate himself with those he fears. Biedermann's 'mask', which he is regularly donning or removing, puts him in a tradition of comic hypocrites which stretches back to Molière and beyond.

Closely related to the use of inconsistency is the use of contradiction, and one of the first amusing touches of the play is an unusual form of it: between a literal statement and a metaphorical understanding of it. In the first lines Anna has protested she cannot throw the pedlar out. Biedermann interprets this to mean she feels sorry for him, and his 'wieso nicht?' is less a question than a challenge – he is almost daring Anna to say she feels sorry for the man at the door. But the tables are turned by Anna's reply: she literally cannot throw the man out because he is so strong. This example of talking at cross-purposes is the first of a large number, but it is different from many others in that the audience too does not suspect the real reasons for Anna's remark. We may smile at the ambiguity of language as much as at Biedermann's harsh interpretation. The same is probably true of the famous exchange between Biedermann and Schmitz:

SCHMITZ: Wer hätte gedacht, ja, wer hätte gedacht, daß es das noch gibt! Heutzutage.
BIEDERMANN: Senf?
SCHMITZ: Menschlichkeit.

As in the exchange between Anna and Biedermann, the speakers are thinking on different levels: Biedermann on the physical, Schmitz on the spiritual, and we are amused by the gulf between the two. Our amusement is heightened by the fact that Biedermann has pretensions on the spiritual plane: he wishes to be admired as a man who *is* 'menschlich', generous and trusting. There is therefore constant comedy through his repeated inability to match the image he wishes to project, and through his obvious preference for the physical. His hypocrisy is so great that he can unselfconsciously contradict himself within a single speech. When he protests loudly to Eisenring that he does not believe in different 'classes' of society, for example (p. 70), he has proved within the next sentence that he vehemently does. And when he shouts at the confused Anna that an item of silverware is not needed, he proves himself incapable of what he claims *is* necessary: 'Menschlichkeit, Brüderlichkeit'. Throughout the play Biedermann fails to say what he really believes, concealing his views behind clichés or even lies. By contrast, the fire-raisers really do mean what they say, and we derive just as much amusement from their open parade of the truth as we do from Biedermann's concealment of it. Ironically, Biedermann cannot believe they are telling the truth. Accustomed as he is to concealing his real views, he does not expect honesty in others.

Another of Frisch's comic devices is use of the incongruous, such as Biedermann's actually protecting the fire-raisers from the police, or his handing over the matches which will lead to his own destruction. Our amusement here may well be tempered by unease over the implications of his stupidity, but this is not the case in the general presentation of the fire-raisers themselves. Both of them embody several features which seem totally out of place in pyromaniacs. Schmitz, for example, is far from being a pathetic pedlar. His clothes are mid-way between those for a prison and those for a circus, he has a tattoo and a leather armband, and his appearance causes Biedermann to drop one of his beloved cigars. Schmitz claims to be a heavyweight wrestler, not a profession with which we associate sensitivity, and yet his taste is if anything more refined than Biedermann's. He obviously takes more delight in fine cigars than Biedermann does, he correctly identifies the wine as Beaujolais, is able to suggest it is slightly too cool, and points out when its temperature is just right (a subtle change from the radio play, when Biedermann made all the observations on the wine). He may munch his food a little loudly, but he knows a good cheese when he sees one and he is very fussy about the condition of his boiled eggs. Eisenring too reveals a taste quite out of keeping with our expectations of a dangerous criminal. He dresses in a tail coat and is constantly trying to teach his accomplice good manners. When asked if he likes goose stuffed with chestnuts, his reply is not immediately affirmative – he asks whether there will be red cabbage too. His sense of grandeur comes out wonderfully as he painstakingly organises the re-laying of the dinner table. The minor details here amuse us most. He doesn't just ask for a fine damask table cloth, but one with a 'frost flower' pattern. And although he first just suggests that finger bowls would be a splendid addition, he then makes it clear he is expecting crystal ones to appear! Biedermann is by contrast an insensitive materialist.

Frisch's comedy of character and situation is heightened through his choice of language. The need to write an earlier version for broadcast (where all is dependent on the ear) may well have concentrated his attention on linguistic effect, for the stage play is undoubtedly his best in terms of dialogue. Humour springs regularly from a contrast between stylistic levels, the sudden changes from serious to frivolous, lofty to banal, pretentious to plain. It also springs from the discrepancy between what characters (especially Biedermann and his wife) *say* and what they actually *mean* or *do*. These figures are in fact trapped by their unthinking use of cliché, which allows them to be manipulated into a position from which they are not prepared to escape. The result is delightful social satire. Take, for example, the scenes in which Schmitz ingratiates himself with Biedermann and then seriously embarrasses Babette. These both produce instances of language being used as a 'social refuge', but the clichés the hosts use are turned against them, and the 'refuge' proves to be a 'prison'. Babette, in desperation, is finally reduced to the ironic protest: 'Sie mißverstehen mich, ach Gott, vollkommen.' On the contrary, Schmitz has understood her only too well. By bluntly stating the truth ('Sie möchten mich los sein?'/'Madame halten mich also für einen Brandstifter –'/ 'Ich weiß: Ich hab kein Benehmen') Schmitz manages to place Babette in a situation which is intolerable to the bourgeois: a situation in which she could be accused of rudeness and heartlessness. Babette would rather suffer a bad-mannered arsonist in her house than be accused of such a thing. So too would her husband, who is determined not to be considered an 'Unmensch'.

If much of the humour of *Biedermann* lies in the author's use of language, a certain part of it lies in the repetition of words, and in particular of phrases, which are repeated by one character or which may be spoken by one and then taken up by another. Dürrenmatt had already used language in this way in *Der Besuch der alten Dame*, and the device is used extensively in the first scene of *Biedermann* (e.g. 'Aufhängen sollte man sie . . . sage und schreibe . . . Ich bin kein Unmensch . . . kommt nicht in Frage . . . etc.)[7] The technique has several functions, not all of which are clearly comic. For example, it may underline aspects of character; it may produce 'mechanical comedy' as a figure repeatedly acts to type and conforms to our expectations; or it may weaken a statement, suggesting the phrase is simply a 'formula' likely to be produced on appropriate occasions. Repetition regularly brings out the hollowness, the hypocrisy, or the folly of the central character.

THE INFLUENCE OF BRECHT

The Chorus may be a device from classical antiquity, yet its appearance can be attributed to a twentieth-century figure: Bertolt Brecht, whose influence on post-war drama was crucial. Brecht had developed his theory of drama well before the war, but he had refined it, and considerably changed its emphases, by the time he met Frisch in 1948. Brecht stayed in Zurich for six months in that year and developed a good relationship with the younger dramatist. Frisch obviously learnt much from their conversations, although he felt intellectually inferior; in addition, his approach to drama, and indeed, to life, was different. Brecht was the great intellectual, approaching everything in terms of ideas; Frisch was more concerned with practical matters and using his own experience.

Brecht absorbed (and sometimes plagiarised) from a wide range of other dramatists and cultures. The main controlling factor in his decision on what would, or would not, suit his purpose, was whether the material or dramatic device would help to establish a 'critical' attitude in his audience – that is, an attitude in which they would *reflect* on what they had seen. Although he later suggested that such emotions as 'pleasure' and 'enjoyment' were a legitimate part of drama, his early writing on what he called 'epic theatre' emphasised that the *rational* response of the spectator was vital. Plays which 'carried away' their spectators by drawing them into an exciting action were not suitable for the modern age. Only if the spectator were detached from the action could he really learn from it, and so the dramatist – and also the actors – must operate with this in mind. The 'Verfremdungseffekt' is one of the most famous concepts associated with this aim. By 'breaking the illusion' and reminding the spectators that they are in a theatre, or by making the events or language of the play seem 'strange', the dramatist does not actually 'alienate' his audience (which would suggest they were out of sympathy with the play), but he seeks rather to 'distance' them, thus encouraging reflection on how to change the social and economic conditions which are destroying those victims of society which the play is presenting.

'Brechtian theatre' has come to suggest three principal features. First, a productive relationship between actor and audience, which is achieved in part through 'Verfremdungseffekte', by various forms of commentary on the action, and by other methods designed to encourage a decision by the audience. This relationship is assisted by a 'bare' stage – or at least a minimum of props. There is no attempt to recreate the appropriate setting, for this might encourage us to identify with the characters. Second, it suggests an 'open' form, that is, an episodically structured play with each scene having its own importance and not being dependent on others. And finally, it suggests some form of political education, in particular through the exposure of bourgeois society.

Frisch's contact with Brecht's views is reflected in several aspects of *Biedermann*. Most obviously, the Chorus is a means of breaking the illusion, commenting on the action, and directly inviting the audience to reflect. The central character has a wholly unrealistic discussion with the Chorus, and later he steps out of role to put a central question to the spectators. (The Dr. phil. also reads a 'speech' to the audience and then goes and sits among them.) The stage does not attempt to create an illusion of reality, for Frisch proposed (in his own design for the set) a 'split stage' of living room and attic immediately above it – reminiscent, perhaps, of medieval morality plays, in which 'heaven' was above. Further, the naming of the characters suggests stylization – Frisch is not concerned to create individuals with whom we can really identify.

Yet for all this, *Biedermann* is more of a traditional play than a Brechtian one: like Dürrenmatt's *Der Besuch der alten Dame*, which appeared a year earlier and which Frisch greatly admired, it is rather a traditional play with Brechtian trappings. Frisch's plot structure is certainly orthodox, with one scene leading quite clearly to the next. There is an exposition, complication and climax. There is a certain amount of suspense too, and the author has taken great pains to entertain his spectators through a good number of traditional comic devices. Further, one could argue that the interventions by the Chorus are not really 'interruptions': they occur at the end of each scene, after we have been 'carried away' by the action which has taken place; and when they figure at a different point – exactly in the middle of the play – their function could be seen as comic rather than monitory. Frisch differs from Brecht in another (although non-dramatic) respect, for the latter tends to see humanity as basically good, forced into evil through the conditions which oppress it. Frisch, on the other hand, seems to see humanity as basically bad. He has a low opinion of all the characters he presents, and the only idealist – the intellectual – is presented as comically helpless.

In some respects the play could even be seen as a rejection of Brecht's dramaturgy and ideology. The sub-title is, after all, a provocative allusion to Brecht's plays of the early thirties, pieces written very strictly to the principle of 'epic theatre' and referred to as 'Lehrstücke'. Frisch, however, specifically states that his version is 'ohne Lehre' – a partial rejection of Brecht, or something rather different?

This paradoxical sub-title can be seen in either of two ways. It may be that Frisch considers the play has the trappings of a didactic drama, but that it nevertheless has no moral. At first sight this may appear ridiculous, but on closer circumspection it does become difficult to say what the moral precisely is. ' "Fate" is not to be confused with "stupidity" ' is hardly a 'moral'. 'Man fears changing himself more than he fears creating disasters' is perhaps more appropriate, but not an issue which the play brings out all that clearly. A more obvious moral might be 'mistrust all beggars!', but this too seems not wholly apt. In a morality play proper the issues are far more clear-cut. Such plays concern themselves more with what the central character *has done* rather than with what he *fails to do*.

The alternative view is that Frisch considers his play does indeed have a moral, but that it will not be grasped. As the Chorus puts it in its final appearance, 'diese Geschichte/ Tötete viele, ach, aber nicht alle,/ *Und änderte gar nichts*'. No one learnt from the disaster, and Frisch's sub-title may be suggesting that no one will learn from his play either. As he once put it in an interview, 'Das signalisiert nur meine Skepsis'.[8] Whatever view of the sub-title we take, Frisch's formulation runs counter to the basic optimism of Brecht and his belief that plays *could* change their audiences.[9]

THE NACHSPIEL

The play was initially produced in Zurich, but for the first German performance Frisch extended the length of the piece by almost a quarter through the addition of a 'postscript'. There was above all a practical reason for this decision: the play as it stands is perfect for an amateur production, but a little too short for a professional evening's entertainment. The division into 'scenes' rather than 'acts' does not help the problem.

For the Zurich performance a short one-act farce was used to fill out the evening, but for the first German production Frisch decided to avoid this unsatisfactory compromise by adding a scene to the main play. Here Biedermann and his wife find themselves in hell, after having been consumed by flames, and they meet the other figures of the play here also. Schmitz and Eisenring turn out to be devils; the 'Polizist' is a visiting angel. The scene is in part a parody of the 'Prolog im Himmel' in Goethe's *Faust*, but those aspects which aroused most interest were lines which clearly attacked West German society of the period. For example, Biedermann and Babette protest their innocence 'compared with others'; they express a desire for 'compensation', despite their guilt; the devils complain that the biggest sinners of all – military officers – are being admitted to heaven; and the city which was destroyed has risen from the ashes even more triumphant than before. These, and a number of other features refer to the materialist 'Wirtschaftswunder' which arose in West Germany of the fifties. The scene exposes the hypocrisy and immorality of the age, and it proves beyond doubt that Biedermann at least has not grasped any 'Lehre' from his experiences.

The 'Nachspiel' may contain a number of subtle and amusing lines neatly adapted from the rest of the play and skilfully linked to the situation of the fifties; in dramatic terms, however, this section is weak. After the high tension of the final scene of the play proper, the after-thought comes as a slow-moving anti-climax. True, its very first performance proved a considerable success, and it has been particularly popular in the Communist countries (for clearly political reasons); but the general western reaction has been unfavourable, and Frisch soon left a decision on whether or not the 'Nachspiel' should be performed to the individual producer. He later decided that he no longer wished to have it performed, nor, indeed, published with the play. It is therefore not included in this edition.

NOTES TO THE INTRODUCTION

1 Two possible exceptions are Eisenring's whistling 'Lili Marlen' as he sets up his fuse, and Babette's brief reference to 'the party'. To a German audience these would establish a connection with World War II, but they are *suggestive* rather than decisive.
2 F. Torberg in the *Neuer Kurier*, 10 June 1958; quoted from I. Springmann, *Max Frisch. Biedermann und die Brandstifter*, p. 68.
3 The entry is actually entitled 'Café Odeon' [a cafe in Zurich at which Frisch recorded his reaction to the news]. Unlike the 'Burleske', which is contained in almost all the volumes of *Materialien*, this entry is available only in the *Tagebuch* itself - *Tagebuch 1946–1949* (Frankfurt, 1950), pp. 242–3.
4 H. Küsel in *Die Gegenwart*, 13 (1958), 695; quoted from I. Springmann, op. cit., p. 66.
5 'Der Chor ist nicht parodistisch gemeint, nur komisch'. One of Frisch's very first comments on the play, featured in the programme for the opening performance. Reprinted in *Materialien* . . ., edited by Walter Schmitz, pp. 66–70.
6 There are other echoes of Hölderlin at various points in the Chorus' speeches. Frisch's exploitation of this speech has been compared to Friedrich Dürrenmatt's handling of it in his play *Der Besuch der alten Dame*, which was published in 1957 and which Frisch greatly admired. For a comparison of the three versions, see I. Springmann, op. cit., pp. 32–3.
7 Ingo Springmann draws attention to the types of repetition, isolating 'whole sentences', 'sentences repeated in abbreviated form', and 'individual, or groups of words'. I find it difficult to

accept Springmann's view that 'die Häufung der Doppelung im Drama zeigt an, daß es sich um besonders affektgeladenes Reden handelt (Annäherung an gesprochene Sprache).' op. cit., p. 5.

8 Transcript in Heinz Ludwig Arnold, *Gespräche mit Schriftstellern*, (Munich, 1975), p. 35.

9 For further details of the relationship between Brecht and Frisch, see Michael Butler's recent study, *The Plays of Max Frisch*. Butler points out that Frisch could not accept either Brecht's belief in the changeability of man or his belief in Marxism. We find in Frisch not a Brechtian optimism, but a deep-seated scepticism, which 'creates an ironic tension, a dark shadow in his otherwise classical stance as an enlightened humanist' (p. 7). Frisch is a 'sceptical moralist', with the hallmark of his plays being a 'radical self-doubt' and a 'search for truth with no confidence that it is attainable' (p. 8).

Butler's study is the best in English to date. In particular, it is helpful for 'placing' Frisch in his Swiss setting (pp. 1–5), for its emphasis on the linguistic 'traps' of the play, and its discussion of the Chorus (pp. 84–95).

SELECT BIBLIOGRAPHY

THE PLAY AND ITS FORERUNNERS

'Burleske' (from the *Tagebuch 1946–1949*), *Gesammelte Werke in zeitlicher Folge*, edited by Hans Mayer, Vol. II, pp. 556–61, Frankfurt am Main, 1976.

Herr Biedermann und die Brandstifter (radio play), *Gesammelte Werke*, Vol. IV, pp. 275–323.

Biedermann und die Brandstifter. Ein Lehrstück ohne Lehre. Mit einem Nachspiel, first published Frankfurt am Main, 1958, but 'Nachspiel' not included in editions after the 13th, i.e. in 1973. Complete text in *Gesammelte Werke*, Vol. IV, pp. 325–415; complete text also available in the earlier Methuen edition by P. K. Ackermann (now out of print).

GENERAL STUDIES OF FRISCH

Hans Bänziger, *Frisch und Dürrenmatt*, 7th ed., Bern, 1976.

Marianne Biedermann, *Das politische Theater von Max Frisch*, Lampertheim, 1974.

Michael Butler, *The Plays of Max Frisch*, London, 1985.

Manfred Durzak, *Dürrenmatt, Frisch, Weiss. Deutsches Drama der Gegenwart zwischen Kritik und Utopie*, 2nd ed., Stuttgart, 1972.

Manfred Jürgensen, *Max Frisch. Die Dramen*, 2nd ed., Bern, 1976.

Eduard Stäuble, *Max Frisch. Gesamtdarstellung seines Werkes*, 4th ed., St. Gallen, 1971.

Alexander Stephan, *Max Frisch*, München, 1983.

Adelheid Weise, *Untersuchungen zur Thematik und Struktur der Dramen von Max Frisch*, Göppingen, 1969.

STUDIES OF THE PLAY:

John T. Brewer, 'Max Frisch's *Biedermann und die Brandstifter* as the documentation of an Author's Frustration', *Germanic Review*, 46 (1971), 119–28.

Hellmuth Karaseck, 'Biedermann und die Brandstifter', a chapter of the author's general study, *Max Frisch*, reprinted in *Über Max Frisch I*, edited by Thomas Beckermann, Frankfurt, 1971, pp. 137–46.

Dieter Herms, 'Max Frisch, *Biedermann und die Brandstifter*', in *Das deutsche Drama vom Expressionismus bis zur Gegenwart. Interpretationen*, edited by Manfred Brauneck, Bamberg, 3rd ed., 1977, pp. 250–8.

Brian Murdoch, 'Teaching Frisch's *Biedermann und die Brandstifter*', *Treffpunkt*, 15, no. 3 (December 1983), 8–15.

For a study of the relationship between Max Mell's *Das Apostelspiel* and the play, see Hans Bänziger, 'Mells *Apostelspiel* und die Parodie *Biedermann*', *Zwischen Protest und Traditionsbewußtsein. Arbeiten zum Werk und zur gesellschaftlichen Stellung Max Frischs*, Bern, 1975, 40–75.

For the relationship between the play and Hugo von Hofmannsthal's *Jedermann*, see Herbert Knust, 'Moderne Variationen des Jedermann-Spiels', first published in the *Helen Adolf Festschrift*, edited by Sheema Z. Buehne, et al., New York, 1968, pp. 309–41, reprinted in *Materialien zu Max Frisch. 'Biedermann und die Brandstifter'*, edited by Walter Schmitz, Frankfurt, 1979, pp. 223–46.

'MATERIALIEN'

Literary 'Materialien' are basically collections of documents relating to a work's genesis, interpretation, and reception. The following are almost all cheap enough for personal purchase, and prices (correct at the time of going to press) are therefore supplied together with advice on general usefulness. Many of these volumes overlap in the 'material' they present, but the amount of interpretation the editors provide varies considerably.

Sybille Heidenreich, *Andorra. Biedermann und die Brandstifter*, Joachim Beyer Verlag, Hollfeld, 4th ed. 1980 (pp. 69–111 on general aspects of the play; fairly basic.) DM 8,80.

Siegfried Hein, *Materialien. Max Frisch. Biedermann und die Brandstifter*, Ernst Klett Verlag, Stuttgart, 1979 (only 39 pp., consisting largely of short extracts from critical studies. A number of useful quotations.) DM 3,50.

Gerda Jordan, *Max Frisch: Biedermann und die Brandstifter*, Verlag Moritz Diesterweg, Frankfurt, 2nd ed., 1983 (55 pp. A fairly full handling of origins, plot, and themes. Recommended.) DM 6,80.

Renate Meurer, Reinhard Meurer, *Max Frisch. Biedermann und die Brandstifter*, R. Oldenbourg Verlag, München, 1983 (82 pp. The most useful, and most recent, of the pamphlets. Fairly detailed analysis of origins, development, plot, characters, language, etc.) DM 12,40.

Theodor Rosebrock, *Erläuterungen zu Max Frisch. Andorra. Biedermann und die Brandstifter*, 9th ed. 1980 (pp. 49–84 on general aspects. Basic points only.) DM 6, 80.

Walter Schmitz, *Materialien zu Max Frisch. 'Biedermann und die Brandstifter'*, suhrkamp taschenbuch 503, Frankfurt, 1979 (328 pp. Considerable (but not exhaustive) information on origins; the author's own pronouncements; first reviews (from Zurich to Moscow); learned interpretations and studies of specific aspects; annotated bibliography.) DM 8,00.

Ingo Springmann, *Max Frisch. Biedermann und die Brandstifter*, Reclam, Universal-Bibliothek 8129, Stuttgart, 1975 (116 pp. and excellent value for its price. Selective coverage of development, critical responses, problems of the play, etc. by means of quotations from the critics.) DM 4,60.

BIEDERMANN UND DIE BRANDSTIFTER

Ein Lehrstück ohne Lehre

PERSONEN:*

Herr Biedermann
Babette, *seine Frau*
Anna, *ein Dienstmädchen*
Schmitz, *ein Ringer*
Eisenring, *ein Kellner*
Ein Polizist
Ein Dr. phil.
Witwe Knechtling

Der Chor, *bestehend aus den Mannen der Feuerwehr*

SZENE: *Eine Stube, ein Dachboden.*

Die Bühne ist finster, dann leuchtet ein Streichholz auf: man sieht das Gesicht von Herrn Biedermann, der sich eine Zigarre anzündet und jetzt, da es heller wird, sich seinerseits umsieht. Ringsum stehen Feuerwehrmänner in Helmen.

BIEDERMANN: Nicht einmal eine Zigarre kann man heutzutage anzünden, ohne an Feuersbrunst zu denken! . . . das ist ja widerlich – *Biedermann verbirgt die rauchende Zigarre und verzieht sich, worauf die Feuerwehr vortritt in der Art des antiken Chors.* * *Eine Turmuhr schlägt: ein Viertel.*

CHOR: Bürger der Vaterstadt,* seht
Wächter der Vaterstadt uns,
Spähend,
Horchend,
Freundlichgesinnte dem freundlichen Bürger –

CHORFÜHRER: Der uns ja schließlich bezahlt.

CHOR: Trefflichgerüstete
Wandeln wir um euer Haus,
Wachsam und arglos zugleich.

CHORFÜHRER: Manchmal auch setzen wir uns,
Ohne zu schlafen jedoch, unermüdlich

CHOR: Spähend,
Horchend,
Daß sich enthülle Verhülltes,
Eh' es zum Löschen zu spät ist,
Feuergefährliches.
Eine Turmuhr schlägt halb.

CHORFÜHRER: Feuergefährlich ist viel,
Aber nicht alles, was feuert, ist Schicksal,
Unabwendbares.

CHOR: Anderes nämlich, Schicksal genannt,
Daß du nicht fragest, wie's kommt,
Städtevernichtendes auch, Ungeheures,
Ist Unfug,

CHORFÜHRER: Menschlicher,

CHOR: Allzumenschlicher,

CHORFÜHRER: Tilgend das sterbliche Bürgergeschlecht.
Eine Turmuhr schlägt: drei Viertel.

CHOR: Viel kann vermeiden Vernunft.

CHORFÜHRER: Wahrlich:

CHOR: Nimmer verdient es der Gott,
Nimmer der Mensch,
Denn der, achtet er Menschliches so,
Nimmer verdient er den Namen
Und nimmer die göttliche Erde,
Die unerschöpfliche,
Fruchtbar und gnädig dem Menschen,
Und nimmer die Luft, die er atmet,
Und nimmer die Sonne –
Nimmer verdient,
Schicksal zu heißen, bloß weil er geschehen:
Der Blödsinn,
Der nimmerzulöschende einst!
Die Turmuhr schlägt: vier Viertel.

CHORFÜHRER: Unsere Wache hat begonnen.
Der Chor setzt sich, während der Stundenschlag tönt: neun Uhr.

SZENE I

Stube
Gottlieb Biedermann sitzt in seiner Stube und liest die Zeitung, eine Zigarre rauchend, und Anna, das Dienstmädchen mit weißem Schürzchen, bringt eine Flasche Wein.

ANNA: Herr Biedermann? – *Keine Antwort.*
Herr Biedermann –
Er legt die Zeitung zusammen.

BIEDERMANN: Aufhängen sollte man sie. Hab ich's nicht immer gesagt? Schon wieder eine Brandstiftung. Und wieder dieselbe Geschichte, sage und schreibe: wieder so ein Hausierer, der sich im Dachboden einnistet, ein harmloser Hausierer. . .
Er nimmt die Flasche.
Aufhängen sollte man sie!
Er nimmt den Korkenzieher.

ANNA: Herr Biedermann –

BIEDERMANN: Was denn?

ANNA: Er ist noch immer da.

BIEDERMANN: Wer?

ANNA: Der Hausierer, der Sie sprechen möchte.

BIEDERMANN: Ich bin nicht zu Hause!

ANNA: Das hab ich ihm gesagt, Herr Biedermann, schon vor einer Stunde. Er sagt, er kenne Sie. Herr Biedermann, ich kann diesen Menschen nicht vor die Tür werfen. Ich kann's nicht!

BIEDERMANN: Wieso nicht?

ANNA: Nämlich er ist sehr kräftig . . .
Biedermann zieht den Korken.

BIEDERMANN: Er soll morgen ins Geschäft kommen.

ANNA: Ich hab's ihm gesagt, Herr Biedermann, schon dreimal, aber das interessiert ihn nicht.

BIEDERMANN: Wieso nicht?

ANNA: Er will kein Haarwasser.*

BIEDERMANN: Sondern?

ANNA: Menschlichkeit . . .
Biedermann riecht am Korken.

BIEDERMANN: Sagen Sie ihm, ich werde ihn eigenhändig vor die Tür werfen, wenn er nicht sofort verschwindet.
Er füllt sorgsam sein Burgunderglas.
Menschlichkeit! . . .
Er kostet den Wein.
Er soll im Flur draußen warten. Ich komme sofort. Wenn er irgend etwas verkauft, ein Traktat oder Rasierklingen, ich bin kein Unmensch, aber – ich bin kein Unmensch, Anna, das wissen Sie ganz genau! – aber es kommt mir keiner ins Haus. Das habe ich Ihnen schon hundertmal gesagt! Und wenn wir drei freie Betten haben, es kommt nicht in Frage, sag ich, nicht in Frage. Man weiß, wohin das führen kann – heutzutage . . . *Anna will gehen und sieht, daß der Fremde eben eingetreten ist: ein Athlet, sein Kostüm erinnert halb an Strafanstalt und halb an Zirkus. Tätowierung am Arm, Lederbinde um die Handgelenke. Anna schleicht hinaus. Der Fremde wartet, bis Biedermann seinen Wein gekostet hat und sich umdreht.*

SCHMITZ: Guten Abend.
Biedermann verliert die Zigarre vor Verblüffung.
Ihre Zigarre, Herr Biedermann –
Er hebt die Zigarre auf und gibt sie Biedermann.

BIEDERMANN: Sagen Sie mal –

SCHMITZ: Guten Abend!

BIEDERMANN: Was soll das heißen? Ich habe dem Mädchen ausdrücklich gesagt, Sie sollen im Flur draußen warten. Wieso – ich muß schon sagen . . . ohne zu klopfen . . .

SCHMITZ: Mein Name ist Schmitz.

BIEDERMANN: Ohne zu klopfen.

SCHMITZ: Schmitz Josef.*
Schweigen
Guten Abend!

BIEDERMANN: Und was wünschen Sie?

SCHMITZ: Herr Biedermann brauchen* keine Angst haben: Ich bin kein Hausierer!

BIEDERMANN: Sondern?

SCHMITZ: Ringer von Beruf.

BIEDERMANN: Ringer?

SCHMITZ: Schwergewicht.

BIEDERMANN: Ich sehe.

SCHMITZ: Das heißt: gewesen.

BIEDERMANN: Und jetzt?

SCHMITZ: Arbeitslos.
Pause
Herr Biedermann brauchen keine Angst haben, ich suche keine Arbeit. Im Gegenteil. Die Ringerei ist mir verleidet . . .*
Bin nur gekommen, weil's draußen so regnet.
Pause
Hier ist's wärmer.
Pause
Hoffentlich stör ich nicht. –
Pause

BIEDERMANN: Rauchen Sie?
Er bietet Zigarren an.

SCHMITZ: Das ist schrecklich, Herr Biedermann, wenn einer so gewachsen ist wie ich. Alle Leute haben Angst vor mir . . .
Danke!
Biedermann gibt ihm Feuer.
Danke.
Sie stehen und rauchen.

BIEDERMANN: Kurz und gut, was wünschen Sie?

SCHMITZ: Mein Name ist Schmitz.

BIEDERMANN: Das sagten Sie schon, ja, sehr erfreut –

SCHMITZ: Ich bin obdachlos.
Er hält die Zigarre unter die Nase und kostet den Duft.
Ich bin obdachlos.

BIEDERMANN: Wollen Sie – ein Stück Brot?

SCHMITZ: Wenn Sie nichts andres haben . . .

BIEDERMANN: Oder ein Glas Wein?

SCHMITZ: Brot und Wein* . . . Aber nur wenn ich nicht störe, Herr Biedermann, nur wenn ich nicht störe!

Biedermann geht zur Tür.

BIEDERMANN: Anna!
Biedermann kommt zurück.

SCHMITZ: Das Mädchen hat mir gesagt, Herr Biedermann will mich persönlich hinauswerfen, aber ich habe gedacht, Herr Biedermann, daß das nicht Ihr Ernst ist . . .
Anna ist eingetreten.

BIEDERMANN: Anna, bringen Sie ein zweites Glas.

ANNA: Sehr wohl.

BIEDERMANN: Und etwas Brot – ja.

SCHMITZ: Und wenn's dem Fräulein nichts ausmacht: etwas Butter. Etwas Käse oder kaltes Fleisch oder so. Nur keine Umstände. Ein paar Gurken, eine Tomate oder so, etwas Senf – was Sie grad haben, Fräulein.*

ANNA: Sehr wohl.

SCHMITZ: Nur keine Umstände!
Anna geht hinaus.

BIEDERMANN: Sie kennen mich, haben Sie dem Mädchen gesagt.

SCHMITZ: Freilich, Herr Biedermann, freilich.

BIEDERMANN: Woher?

SCHMITZ: Nur von Ihrer besten Seite, Herr Biedermann, nur von Ihrer besten Seite. Gestern abend am Stammtisch,* ich weiß, Herr Biedermann haben mich gar nicht bemerkt in der Ecke, die ganze Wirtschaft hat sich gefreut, Herr Biedermann, jedes Mal, wenn Sie mit der Faust auf den Tisch geschlagen haben.

BIEDERMANN: Was habe ich denn gesagt?

SCHMITZ: Das Einzigrichtige.
Er raucht seine Zigarre, dann:
Aufhängen sollte man sie. Alle. Je rascher, um so besser. Aufhängen. Diese Brandstifter nämlich . . .
Biedermann bietet einen Sessel an.

BIEDERMANN: Bitte. –
Schmitz setzt sich.

SCHMITZ: Männer wie Sie, Herr Biedermann, das ist's, was wir brauchen!

BIEDERMANN: Jaja, gewiß, aber –

SCHMITZ: Kein Aber, Herr Biedermann, kein Aber! Sie sind noch vom alten Schrot und Korn,* Sie haben noch eine positive Einstellung. Das kommt davon.*

BIEDERMANN: Gewiß –

SCHMITZ: Sie haben noch Zivilcourage.*

BIEDERMANN: Sicher –

SCHMITZ: Das kommt eben davon.

BIEDERMANN: Wovon?

SCHMITZ: Sie haben noch ein Gewissen, das spürte die ganze Wirtschaft, ein regelrechtes Gewissen.

BIEDERMANN: Jaja, natürlich –

SCHMITZ: Herr Biedermann, das ist gar nicht natürlich. Heutzutage. Im Zirkus, wo ich gerungen hab, zum Beispiel – und drum, sehn Sie, ist er dann auch niedergebrannt, der ganze Zirkus! – unser Direktor zum Beispiel, der* hat gesagt: Sie können mir, Sepp!* – ich heiße doch Josef . . . Sie können mir! hat er gesagt: Wozu soll ich ein Gewissen haben? Wörtlich. Was ich brauche,

um mit meinen Bestien fertigzuwerden, das ist 'ne Peitsche. Wörtlich! So einer war das. Gewissen! hat er gelacht: Wenn einer ein Gewissen hat, so ist es meistens ein schlechtes. . .
Er raucht genußvoll.
Gott hab ihn selig.*

BIEDERMANN: Das heißt, er ist tot?

SCHMITZ: Vebrannt mit seinem ganzen Plunder . . .
Eine Standuhr schlägt neun.

BIEDERMANN: Versteh nicht, was das Mädchen so lange macht!

SCHMITZ: Ich hab Zeit. -
Es gibt sich, daß sie einander plötzlich in die Augen blicken.*
Sie haben auch kein freies Bett im Haus, Herr Biedermann, das Mädchen sagte es schon -

BIEDERMANN: Warum lachen Sie?

SCHMITZ: Leider kein freies Bett! das sagen nämlich alle, kaum daß ein Obdachloser - und dabei will ich gar kein Bett.

BIEDERMANN: Nein?

SCHMITZ: Ich bin's gewohnt, Herr Biedermann, auf dem Boden zu schlafen. Mein Vater war Köhler.* Ich bin's gewohnt . . .
Er raucht vor sich hin.
Kein Aber, Herr Biedermann, kein Aber! sag ich: Sie sind keiner von denen, der in der Wirtschaft ein großes Maul verreißt, weil er Schiß hat.* Ihnen glaub ich's. Leider kein freies Bett! - das sagen alle - aber Ihnen, Herr Biedermann, glaub ich aufs Wort . . . Wo führt das noch hin, wenn keiner mehr dem andern glaubt? Ich sag immer: Wo führt das noch hin, Kinder! jeder hält den andern für einen Brandstifter, nichts als Mißtrauen in der Welt. Oder hab ich nicht recht? Das spürte die ganze Wirtschaft, Herr Biedermann: Sie glauben noch an das Gute in den Menschen

und in sich selbst. Oder hab ich nicht recht? Sie sind der erste Mensch in dieser Stadt, der unsereinen* nicht einfach wie einen Brandstifter behandelt –

BIEDERMANN: Hier ist ein Aschenbecher.

SCHMITZ: Oder hab ich nicht recht?
Er schlägt sorgsam die Asche seiner Zigarre ab.
Die meisten Leute heutzutage glauben nicht an Gott, sondern an die Feuerwehr.

BIEDERMANN: Was wollen Sie damit sagen?

SCHMITZ: Die Wahrheit.
Anna bringt ein Tablettchen.

ANNA: Kaltes Fleisch haben wir keins.

SCHMITZ: Das genügt, Fräulein, das genügt – nur den Senf haben Sie noch vergessen.

ANNA: Entschuldigung!
Anna geht hinaus.

BIEDERMANN: Essen Sie! –
Biedermann füllt die Gläser.

SCHMITZ: Nicht überall, Herr Biedermann, wird man so empfangen. Das kann ich Ihnen sagen! Ich habe schon Dinge erlebt – Kaum tritt unsereiner über die Schwelle, Mann ohne Krawatte, obdachlos, hungrig: Nehmen Sie Platz! heißt es, und hintenherum rufen sie die Polizei. Was finden Sie dazu? Ich frage nach einem Obdach, nichts weiter, ein braver Ringer, der sein Leben lang gerungen hat; da packt so ein Herr, der noch nie gerungen hat, unsereinen am Kragen – Wieso? frag ich und dreh mich bloß um, bloß um ihn anzublicken, schon hat er die Schulter gebrochen.*
Er nimmt das Glas.
Prost!
Sie trinken, und Schmitz beginnt zu futtern.

BIEDERMANN: Es ist halt so eine Sache, mein Herr, heutzutage. Keine Zeitung kann man mehr aufschlagen: Schon

wieder so eine Brandstifterei! Und wieder die alte Geschichte, sage und schreibe: Wieder ein Hausierer, der um Obdach bittet, und am andern Morgen steht das Haus in Flammen . . . Ich meine nur – offengesprochen: Ich kann ein gewisses Mißtrauen schon verstehen.
Er greift zu einer Zeitung.
Hier: bitte!
Er legt ihm die offene Zeitung neben den Teller.

SCHMITZ: Ich hab's gelesen.

BIEDERMANN: Ein ganzer Stadtteil.
Er erhebt sich, um es Schmitz zu zeigen.
Hier: lesen Sie das!
Schmitz futtert und liest und trinkt.

SCHMITZ: Beaujolais?

BIEDERMANN: Ja.

SCHMITZ: Dürfte noch etwas wärmer sein . . .
Er liest über den Teller hinweg.
»– scheint es, daß die Brandstiftung nach dem gleichen Muster geplant und durchgeführt worden ist wie schon das letzte Mal.«
Sie geben einander einen Blick.

BIEDERMANN: Ist das nicht unglaublich?!
Schmitz legt die Zeitung weg.

SCHMITZ: Drum les ich ja keine Zeitungen.

BIEDERMANN: Wie meinen Sie das?

SCHMITZ: Weil's immer wieder dasselbe ist.

BIEDERMANN: Jaja, mein Herr, natürlich, aber – das ist doch keine Lösung, mein Herr, einfach keine Zeitung lesen; schließlich und endlich muß man doch wissen, was einem bevorsteht.

SCHMITZ: Wozu?

BIEDERMANN: Einfach so.

SCHMITZ: Es kommt ja doch, Herr Biedermann, es kommt ja doch!

Er riecht an der Wurst.
Gottesgericht.*
Er schneidet sich Wurst ab.

BIEDERMANN: Meinen Sie?
Anna bringt den Senf.

SCHMITZ: Danke, Fräulein, danke!

ANNA: Sonst noch etwas?

SCHMITZ: Heute nicht.
Anna bleibt bei der Türe.
Senf ist nämlich meine Leibspeise –
Er drückt Senf aus der Tube.

BIEDERMANN: Wieso Gottesgericht?!

SCHMITZ: Weiß ich's . . .*
Er futtert und blickt nochmals in die Zeitung.
»– scheint es den Sachverständigen, daß die Brandstiftung nach dem gleichen Muster geplant und durchgeführt worden ist wie schon das letzte Mal.«
Er lacht kurz, dann füllt er sein Glas mit Wein.

ANNA: Herr Biedermann?

BIEDERMANN: Was denn?

ANNA: Herr Knechtling möchte Sie sprechen.

BIEDERMANN: Knechtling? Jetzt? Knechtling?

ANNA: Er sagt –

BIEDERMANN: Kommt nicht in Frage.

ANNA: Er könne Sie gar nicht verstehen –

BIEDERMANN: Wozu muß er mich verstehen?

ANNA: Er habe eine kranke Frau und drei Kinder –

BIEDERMANN: Kommt nicht in Frage! sag ich.
Er ist aufgestanden vor Ungeduld.
Herr Knechtling! Herr Knechtling! Herr Knechtling soll mich gefälligst in Ruh lassen, Herrgott nochmal, oder er soll einen Anwalt nehmen. Bitte! Ich habe Feierabend.*
Herr Knechtling! Ich verbitte mir dieses Getue wegen einer

Kündigung. Lächerlich! Und dabei gibt's heutzutage Versicherungen wie noch nie in der Geschichte der Menschheit . . . Ja! Soll er* einen Anwalt nehmen. Bitte! Ich werde auch einen Anwalt nehmen. Beteiligung an seiner Erfindung. Soll er sich unter den Gasherd legen oder einen Anwalt nehmen - bitte! - wenn Herr Knechtling es sich leisten kann, einen Prozeß zu verlieren oder zu gewinnen. Bitte! Bitte!
Er beherrscht sich mit Blick auf Schmitz.
Sagen Sie Herrn Knechtling: Ich habe Besuch.
Anna geht hinaus.
Sie entschuldigen!

SCHMITZ: Sie sind hier zu Haus, Herr Biedermann.

BIEDERMANN: Schmeckt es denn?
Er setzt sich und schaut zu, wie der Gast genießt.

SCHMITZ: Wer hätte gedacht, ja, wer hätte gedacht, daß es das noch gibt! Heutzutage.

BIEDERMANN: Senf?

SCHMITZ: Menschlichkeit.
Er schraubt die Tube wieder zu.
Ich meine nur so: Daß Sie mich nicht einfach am Kragen packen, Herr Biedermann, um unsereinen einfach auf die Straße zu werfen - hinaus in den Regen! - sehen Sie, das ist's, Herr Biedermann, was wir brauchen: Menschlichkeit.
Er nimmt die Flasche und gießt sich ein.
Vergelt's Gott.* *Er trinkt und genießt es sichtlich.*

BIEDERMANN: Sie müssen jetzt nicht denken, Herr Schmitz, daß ich ein Unmensch sei -

SCHMITZ: Herr Biedermann!

BIEDERMANN: Frau Knechtling nämlich behauptet das!

SCHMITZ: Wenn Sie ein Unmensch wären, Herr Biedermann, dann würden Sie mir heute nacht kein Obdach geben, das ist mal klar.

BIEDERMANN: Nicht wahr?

SCHMITZ: Und wenn's auch nur auf dem Dachboden ist.
Er stellt das Glas nieder.
Jetzt ist er richtig, unser Wein.
Es klingelt an der Haustür.
Polizei – ?

BIEDERMANN: Meine Frau –

SCHMITZ: Hm.
Es klingelt nochmals.

BIEDERMANN: Kommen Sie! . . . Aber unter einer Bedingung, mein Herr: Kein Lärm! Meine Frau ist herzkrank –
Man hört Frauenstimmen draußen, und Biedermann winkt dem Schmitz, daß er sich beeile, und hilft, Tablettchen und Glas und Flasche werden mitgenommen, sie gehen auf Fußspitzen nach rechts, wo aber der Chor sitzt.

BIEDERMANN: Sie entschuldigen!*
Er steigt über die Bank.

SCHMITZ: Sie entschuldigen!
Er steigt über die Bank, und sie verschwinden, während von links Frau Biedermann in die Stube tritt, begleitet von Anna, die ihr die Sachen abnimmt.

BABETTE: Wo ist mein Mann? Sie wissen, Anna, sir sind keine Spießer:* Sie können einen Schatz haben, aber ich will nicht, Anna, daß Sie ihn im Haus verstecken.

ANNA: Frau Biedermann, ich hab aber keinen.

BABETTE: Und wem gehört das rostige Fahrrad, das unten neben unsrer Haustüre steht? Ich bin ja zu Tod erschrocken –

Dachboden
Biedermann knipst das Licht an, man sieht den Dachboden, er winkt dem Schmitz, daß er eintreten soll, es wird nur geflüstert.

BIEDERMANN: Hier ist der Schalter . . . Wenn Sie kalt haben, irgendwo gibt's ein altes Schaffell,* glaub ich – aber leise, Herrgott nochmal . . . Ziehn Sie die Schuhe aus!

Schmitz stellt das Tablettchen ab und zieht einen Schuh aus.

Herr Schmitz –

SCHMITZ: Herr Biedermann?

BIEDERMANN: Sie versprechen es mir aber: Sie sind aber wirklich kein Brandstifter?

Schmitz muß lachen. *

Scht!

Er nickt gut' Nacht, geht hinaus und macht die Türe zu, Schmitz zieht den anderen Schuh aus.

Stube

Babette hat etwas gehört und horcht, sie blickt entsetzt, dann plötzlich Erleichterung, sie wendet sich an den Zuschauer. *

BABETTE: Mein Mann, der Gottlieb, hat mir versprochen, jeden Abend persönlich auf den Dachboden zu gehen, um persönlich nachzuschauen, ob kein Brandstifter da ist. Ich bin ihm dankbar. Sonst könnte ich nämlich die halbe Nacht lang nicht schlafen . . .

Dachboden

Schmitz geht zum Schalter, jetzt in Socken, und löscht das Licht.

Chor

Bürger der Vaterstadt, seht
Wachen uns,* Wächter der Unschuld,
Arglos noch immer,
Freundlichgesinnte der schlafenden Stadt,
Sitzend,
Stehend –

CHORFÜHRER: Manchmal eine Pfeife stopfend zur Kurzweil.*

CHOR: Spähend,
Horchend,
Daß nicht ein Feuer aus traulichen Dächern
Lichterloh

Tilge die Vaterstadt uns.*
Ein Turmuhr schlägt drei.

CHORFÜHRER: Jedermann weiß, daß wir da sind, und weiß:
Anruf genügt.*
Er stopft sich die Pfeife.

CHOR: Wer denn macht Licht in der Stube
Um diese Stunde?
Wehe, in nervenzerrüttetem Zustand
Schlaflos-unselig
Seh ich die Gattin.
Babette erscheint im Morgenrock.

BABETTE: Da hustet einer! . . .
Man hört Schnarchen.
Gottlieb! Hörst du's denn nicht?
Man hört Husten.
Da ist doch einer! . . .
Man hört Schnarchen.
Männer! dann nehmen sie einfach ein Schlafpulver.*
Eine Turmuhr schlägt vier.

CHORFÜHRER: 's ist vier Uhr.
Babette löscht das Licht wieder.

CHORFÜHRER: Aber ein Anruf kam nicht.
Er steckt die Pfeife wieder ein, es wird hell im Hintergrund.

CHOR: Strahl der Sonne,*
Wimper, o göttlichen Auges,
Aufleuchtet noch einmal Tag
Über den traulichen Dächern der Stadt.
Heil uns!
Nichts ist geschehen der nächtlichen Stadt,
Heute noch nichts . . .
Heil uns!
Der Chor setzt sich.

SZENE 2

Stube
Biedermann steht in Mantel und Hut, Ledermappe unterm Arm, trinkt seinen Morgenkaffee und spricht zur Stube hinaus.

BIEDERMANN: – zum letzten Mal: Er ist kein Brandstifter.

STIMME: Woher weißt du das?

BIEDERMANN: Ich habe ihn ja selbst gefragt . . . Und überhaupt: Kann man eigentlich nichts anderes mehr denken in dieser Welt? Das ist ja zum Verrücktwerden, ihr mit euren Brandstiftern die ganze Zeit –
Babette kommt mit einem Milchkrug.
Zum Verrücktwerden!

BABETTE: Schrei mich nicht an.

BIEDERMANN: Ich schrei nicht dich an, Babette, ich schreie ganz allgemein.
Sie gießt Milch in seine Tasse.
Ich muß ja gehn!
Er trinkt seinen Kaffee, der zu heiß ist.
Wenn man jedermann für einen Brandstifter hält, wo führt das hin? Man muß auch ein bißchen Vertrauen haben, Babette, ein bißchen Vertrauen –
Er blickt auf seine Armbanduhr.

BABETTE: Du bist zu gutmütig. Das mach ich nicht mit, Gottlieb. Du läßt dein Herz sprechen, während ich die ganze Nacht nicht schlafen kann . . . ich will ihm ein Frühstück geben, aber dann, Gottlieb, schick ich ihn auf den Weg.

BIEDERMANN: Tu das.

BABETTE: In aller Freundlichkeit, weiß du, ohne zu kränken.

BIEDERMANN: Tu das.
Er stellt die Tasse hin.
Ich muß zum Rechtsanwalt.
Er gibt Babette einen Gewohnheitskuß, in diesem Augenblick erscheint Schmitz, der ein Schaffell trägt; sie sehen ihn noch nicht.

BABETTE: Warum hast du Knechtling entlassen?

BIEDERMANN: Weil ich ihn nicht mehr brauche.

BABETTE: Du warst immer so zufrieden mit ihm.

BIEDERMANN: Das ist es ja, was er ausnutzen will. Beteiligung an seiner Erfindung! Und dabei weiß Knechtling ganz genau, was unser Haarwasser ist: eine kaufmännische Leistung, aber keine Erfindung. Lächerlich! Die guten Leute, die unser Haarwasser auf die Glatze streichen, könnten ebensogut ihren eigenen Harn –

BABETTE: Gottlieb!

BIEDERMANN: Es ist aber auch wahr!
Er vergewissert sich, ob er alles in der Mappe hat.
Ich bin zu gutmütig, du hast recht: Diesem Knechtling werde ich die Kehle schon umdrehn.*
Er will gehen und sieht Schmitz.*

SCHMITZ: Guten Morgen, die Herrschaften!

BIEDERMANN: Herr Schmitz –
Schmitz streckt ihm die Hand hin.

SCHMITZ: – Sagen Sie doch einfach Sepp!
Biedermann gibt seine Hand nicht.

BIEDERMANN: meine Frau wird mit Ihnen sprechen, Herr Schmitz. Ich muß gehen. Leider. Ich wünsche Ihnen aber alles Gute . . .
Er schüttelt dem Schmitz die Hand.
Alles Gute, Sepp, alles Gute!
Biedermann geht weg.

SCHMITZ: Alles Gute, Gottlieb, alles Gute!
Babette starrt ihn an.
Ihr Mann heißt doch Gottlieb? . . .

BABETTE: Wie haben Sie geschlafen?

SCHMITZ: Danke, kalt. Aber ich habe mir gestattet, Madame, das Schaffell zu nehmen – Erinnert mich an meine Jugend in den Köhlerhütten . . . Ja – Bin die Kälte gewohnt . . .

BABETTE: Ihr Frühstück ist bereit.

SCHMITZ: ·Madame!
Sie weist ihm den Sessel an.
Das kann ich nicht annehmen!
Sie füllt seine Tasse.

BABETTE: Sie müssen tüchtig essen, Sepp. Sie haben sicherlich einen langen Weg vor sich.

SCHMITZ: Wieso?
Sie weist ihm nochmals den Sessel an.

BABETTE: Nehmen Sie ein weiches Ei?

SCHMITZ: Zwei.

BABETTE: Anna!

SCHMITZ: Sie sehen, Madame, ich fühl mich schon wie zu Haus . . . Ich bin so frei –
Er setzt sich, Anna ist eingetreten.

BABETTE: Zwei weiche Eier.

ANNA: Sehr wohl.

SCHMITZ: Dreieinhalb Minuten.

ANNA: Sehr wohl.
Anna will gehen.

SCHMITZ: Fräulein!
Anna steht in der Tür.
Guten Tag!

ANNA: Tag.
Anna geht hinaus.

SCHMITZ: Wie das Fräulein mich ansieht! Verdammt nochmal! Wenn's auf die ankäme, ich glaub, ich stünde draußen im strömenden Regen.
Babette gießt Kaffee ein.

BABETTE: Herr Schmitz –

SCHMITZ: Ja?

BABETTE: Wenn ich offen sprechen darf: –

SCHMITZ: Sie zittern, Madame!?

BABETTE: Herr Schmitz –

SCHMITZ: Was bekümmert Sie?

BABETTE: Hier ist Käse.

SCHMITZ: Danke.

BABETTE: Hier ist Marmelade.

SCHMITZ: Danke.

BABETTE: Hier ist Honig.

SCHMITZ: Eins nach dem andern, Madame, eins nach dem andern!
Er lehnt zurück und ißt sein Butterbrot, zum Hören bereit.
Was ist's?

BABETTE: Rundheraus, Herr Schmitz –

SCHMITZ: Sagen Sie doch einfach Sepp.

BABETTE: Rund heraus –

SCHMITZ: Sie möchten mich los sein?

BABETTE: Nein, Herr Schmitz, nein! so würd ich es nicht sagen –

SCHMITZ: Wie würden Sie's denn sagen?
Er nimmt Käse.
Tilsiter ist nämlich meine Leibspeis.*
Er lehnt wieder zurück und futtert, zum Hören bereit.
Madame halten mich also für einen Brandstifter –

BABETTE: Mißverstehen Sie mich nicht! Was hab ich denn gesagt? Nichts liegt mir ferner, Herr Schmitz, als Sie zu kränken. Ehrenwort! Sie haben mich ganz verwirrt. Wer redet denn von Brandstiftern! Ich beklage mich ja in keiner Weise, Herr Schmitz, über Ihr Benehmen –
Schmitz legt das Besteck nieder.

SCHMITZ: Ich weiß: Ich hab kein Benehmen.

BABETTE: Nein, Herr Schmitz, das ist es nicht –

SCHMITZ: Ein Mensch, der schmatzt –

BABETTE: Unsinn –

SCHMITZ: Das haben sie mir schon im Waisenhaus immer gesagt: Schmitz, schmatze nicht!

Sie nimmt die Kanne, um Kaffee einzugießen.

BABETTE: Sie mißverstehen mich, ach Gott, vollkommen.

Er hält die Hand auf seine Tasse.

SCHMITZ: Ich geh.

BABETTE: Herr Schmitz –

SCHMITZ: Ich geh.

BABETTE: Noch eine Tasse?

Er schüttelt den Kopf.

BABETTE: Eine halbe?

Er schüttelt den Kopf.

So dürfen Sie nicht gehen, Herr, ich habe Sie nicht kränken wollen, Herr, ich habe doch kein Wort gesagt, daß Sie schmatzen!

Er erhebt sich.

Habe ich Sie gekränkt?

Er faltet die Serviette zusammen.

SCHMITZ: Was können Madame dafür, daß ich kein Benehmen habe! Mein Vater war Köhler. Woher soll unsereiner ein Benehmen haben! Hungern und frieren, Madame, das macht mir nichts, aber – keine Bildung, Madame, kein Benehmen, Madame, keine Kultur . . .

BABETTE: Ich versteh.

SCHMITZ: Ich geh.

BABETTE: Wohin?

SCHMITZ: Hinaus in den Regen . . .

BABETTE: Ach Gott.

SCHMITZ: Bin ich gewohnt.

BABETTE: Herr Schmitz . . . Blicken Sie mich nicht so an! – Ihr Vater war Köhler, das sehe ich doch ein, Herr Schmitz, Sie haben sicherlich eine harte Jugend gehabt –

SCHMITZ: Überhaupt keine, Madame.

Er senkt den Blick und fingert an seinen Fingern herum.
Überhaupt keine. Ich zählte sieben Jahr, als meine Mutter starb . . .
Er dreht sich und wischt sich die Augen.

BABETTE: Sepp! – aber Sepp . . .
Anna kommt und bringt die weichen Eier.

ANNA: Sonst noch etwas?
Anna bekommt keine Antwort und geht hinaus.

BABETTE: Ich schicke Sie gar nicht fort, mein Herr, das habe ich ja gar nicht gesagt. Was habe ich denn gesagt? Sie mißverstehen mich wirklich, Herr Schmitz, das ist ja furchtbar. Was kann ich denn tun, daß Sie mir glauben?
Sie faßt ihn (nicht ohne Zögern) am Ärmel.
Kommen Sie, Sepp, essen Sie!
Schmitz setzt sich wieder an den Tisch.
Wofür halten Sie uns! Ich habe nicht bemerkt, daß Sie schmatzen, Ehrenwort! Und wenn schon: Wir geben nichts auf Äußerlichkeiten, Herr Schmitz, das müssen Sie doch spüren, Herr Schmitz, wir sind nicht so . . .
Er köpft sein Ei.

SCHMITZ: Vergelt's Gott!

BABETTE: Hier ist Salz.
Er löffelt das Ei.

SCHMITZ: 's ist wahr, Madame haben mich ja gar nicht fortgeschickt, kein Wort davon, 's ist wahr. Bitte um Entschuldigung, daß ich Madame so mißverstanden habe . . .

BABETTE: Ist es denn richtig, das Ei?

SCHMITZ: Etwas weich . . . Bitte sehr um Entschuldigung.
Er hat es ausgelöffelt.
Was haben Sie denn sagen wollen, Madame, vorher als Sie sagten: Rundheraus!

BABETTE: Ja, was hab ich eigentlich sagen wollen . . .
Er köpft das zweite Ei.

SCHMITZ: Vergelt's Gott.

Er löffelt das zweite Ei.

Der Willi, der sagt immer, das gibt's gar nicht mehr: die private Barmherzigkeit. Es gibt heutzutage keine feinen Leute mehr. Verstaatlichung! Es gibt keine Menschen mehr. Sagt er! - drum geht die Welt in den Eimer* - drum! . . .

Er salzt das Ei.

Der wird Augen machen! - wenn er ein solches Frühstück bekommt, der wird Augen machen! . . . Der Willi!

Es klingelt an der Haustür.

SCHMITZ: Vielleicht ist er das.

Es klingelt an der Haustür.

BABETTE: Wer ist der Willi?

SCHMITZ: Der hat Kultur, Madame, Sie werden sehen, der ist doch Kellner gewesen damals im Metropol,* bevor's niedergebrannt ist, das Metropol -

BABETTE: Niedergebrannt?

SCHMITZ: Oberkellner.

Anna ist eingetreten.

BABETTE: Wer ist's?

ANNA: Ein Herr.

BABETTE: Und was will er?

ANNA: Von der Feuerversicherung, sagt er, nämlich er müsse sich das Haus ansehen.

Babette erhebt sich.

Er trägt einen Frack -

Babette und Anna gehen hinaus, Schmitz gießt sich Kaffee ein.

SCHMITZ: Der Willi!

Chor

Nun aber sind es schon zwei,
Die unsern Argwohn erwecken,
Fahrräder nämlich, verrostete, die
Jemand gehören, doch wem?

CHORFÜHRER: Eines seit gestern, das andre seit heut.

CHOR: Wehe!

CHORFÜHRER: Wieder ist Nacht, und wir wachen.
Eine Turmuhr schlägt.

CHOR: Viel sieht, wo nichts ist, der Ängstliche,*
Den nämlich schreckt schon der eigene Schatten,
Kampfmutig findet ihn jedes Gerücht,
So daß er strauchelt,
So, schreckhaft, lebt er dahin,
Bis es eintritt:
In seine Stube.
Die Turmuhr schlägt.

CHORFÜHRER: Daß sie das Haus nicht verlassen, die zwei,
Wie soll ich's deuten?
Die Turmuhr schlägt.

CHOR: Blinder als blind ist der Ängstliche,
Zitternd vor Hoffnung, es sei nicht das Böse,
Freundlich empfängt er's,
Wehrlos, ach, müde der Angst,
Hoffend das beste . . .
Bis es zu spät ist.
Die Turmuhr schlägt.

CHOR: Wehe!
Der Chor setzt sich.

SZENE 3

Dachboden
Schmitz, immer im Kostüm des Ringers, und der Andere, der seinen Frack ausgezogen hat und nur die weiße Weste trägt, sind dabei, Fässer in den Estrich zu rollen, Fässer aus Blech, wie sie zum Transport von Benzin üblich sind, alles so leise als möglich; beide haben ihre Schuhe ausgezogen.*

DER ANDERE: Leise! Leise!

SCHMITZ: Und wenn er auf die Idee kommt und die Polizei ruft?

DER ANDERE: Vorwärts!

SCHMITZ Was dann?

DER ANDERE: Langsam! Langsam . . . Halt.
Sie haben das Faß zu den andern gerollt, die schon im Dämmerdunkel stehen; der Andere nimmt Putzfäden, um sich die Finger zu wischen.

DER ANDERE: Wieso soll er die Polizei rufen?

SCHMITZ: Wieso nicht?

DER ANDERE: Weil er selber strafbar ist.
Man hört Gurren von Tauben. *
's ist leider Tag, gehn wir schlafen!
Er wirft die Putzfäden weg.
Jeder Bürger ist strafbar, genaugenommen, von einem gewissen Einkommen an. Mach dir keine Sorge! . . .
Es klopft an der verriegelten Tür.

BIEDERMANN: Aufmachen! Aufmachen!
Es poltert und rüttelt. *

DER ANDERE: Das tönt aber nicht nach Frühstück.

BIEDERMANN: Aufmachen! sag ich. Sofort!

SCHMITZ: So war er noch nie.
Es poltert mehr und mehr. Der Andere zieht seinen Frack an. Ohne Hast, aber flink. Er zieht die Krawatte zurecht und wischt sich den Staub ab, dann öffnet er die Tür: – eintritt Biedermann im Morgenrock, wobei er den neuen Gesellen, da dieser hinter der aufgehenden Tür steht, nicht bemerkt.

BIEDERMANN: Herr Schmitz!

SCHMITZ: Guten Morgen, Herr Biedermann, guten Morgen, hoffentlich hat Sie das blöde Gepolter nicht geweckt –

BIEDERMANN: Herr Schmitz!

SCHMITZ: Soll nie wieder vorkommen.

BIEDERMANN: Sie verlassen mein Haus. –
Pause
Ich sage: Sie verlassen mein Haus!

SCHMITZ: Wann?

BIEDERMANN: Sofort.

SCHMITZ: Wieso?

BIEDERMANN: Oder meine Frau (ich kann und ich werde es nicht hindern!) ruft die Polizei.

SCHMITZ: Hm.

BIEDERMANN: Und zwar sofort!
Pause
Worauf warten Sie?
Schmitz, stumm, nimmt seine Schuhe.
Ich will keine Diskussion!

SCHMITZ: Ich sag ja gar nichts.

BIEDERMANN: Wenn Sie meinen, Herr Schmitz, ich lasse mir alles gefallen, bloß weil Sie ein Ringer sind – ein solches Gepolter die ganze Nacht –
Er zeigt mit gestrecktem Arm zur Tür.
Hinaus! Hinaus! sag ich. Hinaus!
Schmitz spricht zum Andern hinüber.

SCHMITZ: So war er noch nie . . .
Biedermann dreht sich um und ist sprachlos.

DER ANDERE: Mein Name ist Eisenring.

BIEDERMANN: Meine Herrn – ?

EISENRING: Wilhelm Maria Eisenring.*

BIEDERMANN: Wieso, meine Herrn, wieso sind Sie plötzlich zwei?
Schmitz und Eisenring blicken einander an.
Ohne zu fragen!

EISENRING: Siehst du.*

BIEDERMANN: Was soll das heißen?

EISENRING: Ich hab's dir ja gesagt. Das macht man nicht, Sepp, du hast kein Benehmen. Ohne zu fragen. Was ist das für eine Art:* – plötzlich sind wir zwei.

BIEDERMANN: Ich bin außer mir.

EISENRING: Siehst du!
Er wendet sich an Biedermann.
Ich hab es ihm gesagt!
Er wendet sich an Schmitz.
Hab ich es dir nicht gesagt?
Schmitz schämt sich.

BIEDERMANN: Was stellen Sie sich eigentlich vor,* meine Herren? Schließlich und endlich,* meine Herren, bin ich der Hauseigentümer. Ich frage: Was stellen Sie sich eigentlich vor?
Pause.

EISENRING: Antworte, wenn der Herr dich fragt!
Pause

SCHMITZ: Der Willi ist doch mein Freund . . .

BIEDERMANN: Was weiter?

SCHMITZ: Wir sind doch zusammen in die Schule gegangen, Herr Biedermann, schon als Kinder . . .

BIEDERMANN: Und?

SCHMITZ: Da hab ich gedacht . . .

BIEDERMANN: Was?

SCHMITZ: Da hab ich gedacht . . .
Pause

EISENRING: Nichts hast du gedacht!
Er wendet sich an Biedermann.
Ich versteh Sie vollkommen, Herr Biedermann. Alles was recht ist, aber schließlich und endlich –
Er schreit Schmitz an.
Meinst du eigentlich, ein Hauseigentümer braucht sich alles gefallen zu lassen?
Er wendet sich an Biedermann.
Der Sepp hat Sie überhaupt nicht gefragt?

BIEDERMANN: Kein Wort!

EISENRING: Sepp –

BIEDERMANN: Kein Wort!

EISENRING: – und dann wunderst du dich, wenn man dich auf die Straße wirft?
Er schüttelt den Kopf und lacht wie über einen Dummkopf.

BIEDERMANN: Es ist nicht zum Lachen, meine Herren. Es ist mir bitterernst, meine Herren. Meine Frau ist herzkrank –

EISENRING: Siehst du!

BIEDERMANN: Meine Frau hat die halbe Nacht nicht geschlafen. Wegen dieser Polterei. Und überhaupt: – Was machen Sie da eigentlich?
Er sieht sich um.
Was, zum Teufel, sollen diese Fässer hier?*
Schmitz und Eisenring sehen dahin, wo keine Fässer sind.
Hier! Bitte! Was ist das?
Er klopft auf ein Faß.
Was ist das?

SCHMITZ: Fässer . . .

BIEDERMANN: Wo kommen die her?

SCHMITZ: Weißt du's, Willi? wo sie herkommen.

EISENRING: Import, es steht drauf.

BIEDERMANN: Meine Herren –

EISENRING: Irgendwo steht's drauf!
Eisenring und Schmitz suchen die Anschrift.

BIEDERMANN: Ich bin sprachlos. Was stellen Sie sich eigentlich vor? Mein ganzer Dachboden voll Fässer – gestapelt, geradezu gestapelt!

EISENRING: Ja eben.*

BIEDERMANN: Was wollen Sie damit sagen?

EISENRING: Der Sepp hat sich verrechnet . . . Zwölf auf fünfzehn Meter! hast du gesagt, und dabei hat er keine hundert Quadratmeter, dieser ganze Dachboden . . . Ich kann meine Fässer nicht auf der Straße lassen, Herr Biedermann, das werden Sie verstehen.

BIEDERMANN: Nichts verstehe ich – *Schmitz zeigt eine Etikette.*

SCHMITZ: Hier, Herr Biedermann, hier ist die Etikette!

BIEDERMANN: Ich bin sprachlos –

SCHMITZ: Hier steht's, wo sie herkommen. Hier.

BIEDERMANN: – einfach sprachlos.
Er betrachtet die Etikette.

Unten
Anna führt einen Polizisten in die Stube.

ANNA: Ich werde ihn rufen.
Sie geht, und der Polizist wartet.

Oben

BIEDERMANN: Benzin!? –

Unten
Anna kommt nochmals zurück.

ANNA: Und worum handelt es sich, Herr Wachtmeister?

POLIZIST: Geschäftlich.
Anna geht, und der Polizist wartet.

Oben

BIEDERMANN: Ist das wahr, meine Herren, ist das wahr?

EISENRING: Was?

BIEDERMANN: Was auf dieser Etikette steht.
Er zeigt ihnen die Etikette.
Wofür halten Sie mich eigentlich? Das ist mir noch nicht vorgekommen. Glauben Sie eigentlich, ich kann nicht lesen?
Sie betrachten die Etikette.
Bitte! –
Er lacht, wie man über eine Unverschämtheit lacht.

Benzin!
Er spricht wie ein Untersuchungsrichter.
Was ist in diesen Fässern?

EISENRING: Benzin.

BIEDERMANN: Machen Sie keine Witze! Ich frage zum letzten Mal, was in diesen Fässern ist. Sie wissen so gut wie ich, daß Benzin nicht auf den Dachboden gehört –
*Er fährt mit dem Finger über ein Faß**
Bitte – da: riechen Sie selbst!
Er hält ihnen den Finger unter die Nase.
Ist das Benzin oder ist das kein Benzin?
Sie schnuppern und blicken einander an.
Antworten Sie!

EISENRING: Es ist.

SCHMITZ: Es ist.

BEIDE: Eindeutig.

BIEDERMANN: Sind Sie eigentlich wahnsinnig? Mein ganzer Dachboden voll Benzin –

SCHMITZ: Drum, Herr Biedermann, rauchen wir auch nicht.

BIEDERMANN: Und das, meine Herren, in dieser Zeit, wo man in jeder Zeitung, die man aufschlägt, gewarnt wird. Was denken Sie sich eigentlich? Meine Frau bekommt einen Schlag, wenn sie das sieht.

EISENRING: Siehst du!

BIEDERMANN: Sagen Sie nicht immer: Siehst du!

EISENRING: Das kannst du einer Frau nicht zumuten,* Sepp, einer Hausfrau, ich kenne die Hausfrauen –
Anna ruft im Treppenhaus.

ANNA: Herr Biedermann! Herr Biedermann!
Biedermann macht die Türe zu.

BIEDERMANN: Herr Schmitz! Herr –

EISENRING: Eisenring.

BIEDERMANN: Wenn Sie diese Fässer nicht augenblicklich aus dem Hause schaffen, aber augenblicklich! sag ich –

EISENRING: Dann rufen Sie die Polizei.

BIEDERMANN: Ja.

SCHMITZ: Siehst du!

Anna ruft im Treppenhaus.

ANNA: Herr Biedermann!

Biedermann flüstert.

BIEDERMANN: Das war mein letztes Wort!

EISENRING: Welches?

BIEDERMANN: Ich dulde kein Benzin in meinem Dachstock. Ein für allemal! Ich dulde es nicht.

Es klopft an die Tür.

Ich komme!

Er öffnet die Tür, um zu gehen, und eintritt ein Polizist.

POLIZIST: Da sind Sie ja, Herr Biedermann, da sind Sie ja. Sie brauchen nicht herunterzukommen, ich will nicht lange stören.

BIEDERMANN: Guten Morgen!

POLIZIST: Guten Morgen!

EISENRING: Morgen . . .

SCHMITZ: Morgen . . .

Schmitz und Eisenring verneigen sich.

POLIZIST: Es handelt sich um einen Unfall –

BIEDERMANN: Um Gottes willen!

POLIZIST: Ein alter Mann, dessen Frau behauptet, er habe bei Ihnen gearbeitet – als Erfinder! – hat sich heute nacht unter den Gashahn gelegt.*

Er sieht in seinem Notizbüchlein nach.

POLIZIST: Knechtling, Johann, wohnhaft Roßgasse 11.

Er steckt das Büchlein ein.

Haben Sie einen solchen gekannt?

BIEDERMANN: Ich –

POLIZIST: Vielleicht ist's Ihnen lieber, Herr Biedermann, wenn wir unter vier Augen* –

BIEDERMANN: Ja.

POLIZIST: Geht ja die Angestellten nichts an!*

BIEDERMANN: Nein –
Er bleibt in der Tür stehen.
Wenn mich jemand sucht, meine Herren, ich bin bei der Polizei. Verstanden? Ich komme sofort.
Schmitz und Eisenring nicken.

POLIZIST: Herr Biedermann –

BIEDERMANN: Gehen wir!

POLIZIST: Was haben Sie denn in diesen Fässern da?

BIEDERMANN: – ich?

POLIZIST: Wenn man fragen darf.

BIEDERMANN: . . . Haarwasser . . .
Er blickt zu Schmitz und Eisenring.

EISENRING: HORMOFLOR.*

SCHMITZ: »Die Männerwelt atmet auf.«

EISENRING: HORMOFLOR.

SCHMITZ: »Versuchen Sie es noch heute.«

EISENRING: »Sie werden es nicht bereuen.«

BEIDE: HORMOFLOR, HORMOFLOR.
Der Polizist lacht.

BIEDERMANN: Ist er tot?
Biedermann und der Polizist gehen.

EISENRING: Eine Seele von Mensch.*

SCHMITZ: Hab ich's nicht gesagt?

EISENRING: Aber von Frühstück kein Wort.

SCHMITZ: So war er noch nie . . .
Eisenring greift in seine Hosentasche.

EISENRING: Hast du die Zündkapsel?
Schmitz greift in seine Hosentasche.

SCHMITZ: So war er noch nie . . .

Chor
Strahl der Sonne,*
Wimper, o göttlichen Auges,
Aufleuchtet noch einmal
Tag
Über den traulichen Dächern der Stadt.

CHORFÜHRER: Heute wie gestern.

CHOR: Heil uns!

CHORFÜHRER: Nichts ist geschehen der schlafenden Stadt.

CHOR: Heil uns!

CHORFÜHRER: Immer noch nichts . . .

CHOR: Heil uns!
Man hört Verkehrslärm, Hupen, Straßenbahn.

CHORFÜHRER: Klug ist und Herr über manche Gefahr,
Wenn er bedenkt, was er sieht,
Der Mensch.
Aufmerkenden Geistes vernimmt er
Zeichen des Unheils
Zeitig genug, wenn er will.

CHOR: Was aber, wenn er nicht will?

CHORFÜHRER: Der, um zu wissen, was droht,*
Zeitungen liest
Täglich zum Frühstück entrüstet
Über ein fernes Ereignis,
Täglich beliefert mit Deutung,
Die ihm das eigene Sinnen erspart,
Täglich erfahrend, was gestern geschah,
Schwerlich durchschaut er, was eben geschieht
Unter dem eigenen Dach: –

CHOR: Unveröffentlichtes!

CHORFÜHRER: Offenkundiges.

CHOR: Hanebüchenes!

CHORFÜHRER: Tatsächliches.

CHOR: Ungern durchschaut er's denn sonst –
Der Chorführer unterbricht mit einem Zeichen der Hand.

CHORFÜHRER: Hier kommt er.
Der Chor schwenkt die Front. *

CHOR: Nichts ist geschehen der schlafenden Stadt,
Heute wie gestern,
Um zu vergessen, was droht,
Stürzt sich der Bürger
Sauber rasiert
In sein Geschäft . . .
Auftritt Biedermann in Mantel und Hut, Mappe im Arm.

BIEDERMANN: Taxi! . . . Taxi? . . . Taxi!
Der Chor steht ihm im Weg.
Was ist los?

CHOR: Wehe!

BIEDERMANN: Sie wünschen?

CHOR: Wehe!

BIEDERMANN: Das sagten Sie schon.

CHOR: Dreimal Wehe!

BIEDERMANN: Wieso?

CHORFÜHRER: Allzuverdächtiges, scheint uns,
Feuergefährliches hat sich enthüllt
Unseren Blicken wie deinen.
Wie soll ich's deuten?
Fässer voll Brennstoff im Dach –
Biedermann schreit.

BIEDERMANN: Was geht das Sie an!
Schweigen
Lassen Sie mich durch. – Ich muß zu meinem Rechtsanwalt. –
Was will man von mir? – Ich bin unschuldig . . .
Biedermann scheint verängstigt.
Soll das ein Verhör sein?
Biedermann zeigt herrenhafte Sicherheit.

Lassen Sie mich durch, ja.*
Der Chor steht reglos.

CHOR: Nimmer geziemt es dem Chor,
Richter zu sein über Bürger, die handeln.

CHORFÜHRER: Der nämlich zusieht* von außen, der Chor,
Leichter begreift er, was droht.

CHOR: Fragend nur, höflich
Noch in Gefahr, die uns schreckt,
Warnend nur, ach kalten Schweißes gefaßt*
Naht sich bekanntlich der Chor,
Ohnmächtig-wachsam, mitbürgerlich,
Bis es zum Löschen zu spät ist,
Feuerwehrgleich.
Biedermann blickt auf seine Armbanduhr.

BIEDERMANN: Ich bin eilig.*

CHOR: Wehe!

BIEDERMANN: Ich weiß wirklich nicht, was Sie wünschen.

CHORFÜHRER: Daß du sie duldest, die Fässer voll Brennstoff,
Biedermann, Gottlieb, wie hast du's gedeutet?

BIEDERMANN: Gedeutet?

CHORFÜHRER: Wissend auch du, wie brennbar die Welt ist,
Biedermann Gottlieb, was hast du gedacht?

BIEDERMANN: Gedacht?
Er mustert den Chor.
Meine Herrn, ich bin ein freier Bürger. Ich kann denken, was ich will. Was sollen diese Fragen? Ich habe das Recht, meine Herrn, überhaupt nichts zu denken - ganz abgesehen davon, meine Herrn: Was unter meinem Dach geschieht - ich muß schon sagen, schließlich und endlich bin ich der Hauseigentümer!

CHOR: Heilig sei Heiliges uns,*
Eigentum,
Was auch entstehe daraus,
Nimmerzulöschendes einst,

Das uns dann alle versengt und verkohlt:
Heilig sei Heiliges uns!

BIEDERMANN: Also. –
Schweigen
Warum lassen Sie mich nicht durch?
Schweigen
Man soll nicht immer das Schlimmste denken. Wo führt das hin! Ich will meine Ruhe und meinen Frieden haben, nichts weiter, und was die beiden Herren betrifft – ganz abgesehen davon, daß ich zur Zeit andere Sorgen habe . . .
Auftritt Babette in Mantel und Hut.
Was willst du hier?

BABETTE: Stör ich?

BIEDERMANN: Ich habe eine Besprechung mit dem Chor.
Babette nickt zum Chor, dann flüstert sie Biedermann ins Ohr.
Natürlich mit Schleife! Das spielt doch keine Rolle, was er kostet, Hauptsache, daß es ein Kranz ist.
Babette nickt zum Chor.

BABETTE: Sie verzeihen, meine Herren. *Babette entfernt sich.*

BIEDERMANN: . . . kurz und gut, meine Herrn, ich habe es satt, Ihr mit euren Brandstiftern! Ich geh an keinen Stammtisch mehr, so satt hab ich's. Kann man eigentlich nichts andres mehr reden heutzutag? Schließlich lebe ich nur einmal. Wenn wir jeden Menschen, ausgenommen uns selbst, für einen Brandstifter halten, wie soll es jemals besser werden? Ein bißchen Vertrauen, Herrgottnochmal, muß man schon haben, ein bißchen guten Willen. Finde ich. Nicht immer nur das Böse sehen. Herrgottnochmal! Nicht jeder Mensch ist ein Brandstifter. Finde ich! Ein bißchen Vertrauen, ein bißchen . . .
Pause
Ich kann nicht Angst haben die ganze Zeit!
Pause
Heute nacht, meinen Sie denn, ich habe ein einziges Auge

geschlossen? Ich bin ja nicht blöd. Benzin ist Benzin! Ich habe mir die allerschwersten Gedanken gemacht - auf den Tisch bin ich gestiegen, um zu horchen, und später sogar auf den Schrank, um mein Ohr an die Zimmerdecke zu legen. Jawohl! Geschnarcht haben sie. Geschnarcht! Mindestens viermal bin ich auf den Schrank gestiegen. Ganz friedlich geschnarcht! . . . Und trotzdem: - Einmal stand ich schon draußen im Treppenhaus, ob Sie's glauben oder nicht, im Pyjama - vor Wut. Ich war drauf und dran, die beiden Halunken zu wecken und auf die Straße zu werfen - mitsamt ihren Fässern! - eigenhändig, rücksichtslos, mitten in der Nacht!

CHOR: Eigenhändig?

BIEDERMANN: Ja.

CHOR: Rücksichtslos?

BIEDERMANN: Ja.

CHOR: Mitten in der Nacht?

BIEDERMANN: Ich war drauf und dran, ja - wäre meine Frau nicht gekommen, die fürchtete, daß ich mich erkälte - drauf und dran!
Er nimmt sich eine Zigarre aus Verlegenheit.

CHORFÜHRER: Wie soll ich's abermals deuten?
Schlaflos verging ihm die Nacht.
Daß sie die Güte des Bürgers mißbrauchen,
Schien es ihm denkbar?*
Argwohn befiel ihn. Wieso?
Biedermann zündet seine Zigarre an.

CHOR: Schwer hat es, wahrlich, der Bürger!
Der nämlich, hart im Geschäft,
Sonst aber Seele von Mensch,
Gerne bereit ist,
Gutes zu tun.

CHORFÜHRER: Wo es ihm paßt.

CHOR: Hoffend, es komme das Gute

Aus Gutmütigkeiten
Der nämlich irrt sich gefährlich.

BIEDERMANN: Was wollen Sie damit sagen?

CHOR: Uns nämlich dünkte, es stinkt nach Benzin.
Biedermann schnuppert.

BIEDERMANN: Also, meine Herren, ich rieche nichts . . .

CHOR: Weh uns!

BIEDERMANN: Rein gar nichts.

CHOR: Weh uns!

CHORFÜHRER: So schon gewohnt ist er bösen Geruch.

CHOR: Weh uns!

BIEDERMANN: Und kommen Sie nicht immer mit diesem Defaitismus, meine Herrn, sagen Sie nicht immer: Weh uns!
Man hört ein Auto hupen.
Taxi! - Taxi!
Man hört, wie ein Auto stoppt.
Sie entschuldigen.
Biedermann geht in Eile weg.

CHOR: Bürger - wohin!?
Man hört, wie ein Auto losfährt.

CHORFÜHRER: Was hat er vor, der Unselige, jetzt?
Ängstlich-verwegen,* so schien mir, und bleich
Lief er davon,
Ängstlich-entschlossen: wozu?
Man hört, wie ein Auto hupt.

CHOR: So schon gewohnt ist er bösen Geruch!
Man hört das Hupen in der Ferne.
Weh uns!

CHORFÜHRER: Weh euch!
Der Chor tritt zurück, ausgenommen der Chorführer, der seine Pfeife nimmt.

CHORFÜHRER: Der die Verwandlungen scheut*

Mehr als das Unheil,
Was kann er tun
Wider das Unheil?
Er folgt dem Chor.

SZENE 4

Dachboden
Eisenring ist allein und arbeitet, indem er Schnur von einem Haspel wickelt und pfeift dazu: Lili Marlen. Er unterbricht sein Pfeifen, um den Zeigfinger* zu nässen, und hält den Zeigfinger durch die Lukarne hinaus, um den Wind zu prüfen.*

Stube
Eintritt Biedermann, gefolgt von Babette, er zieht seinen Mantel aus und wirft die Mappe hin, die Zigarre im Mund.

BIEDERMANN: Tu, was ich dir sage.

BABETTE: Eine Gans?

BIEDERMANN: Eine Gans.
Er zieht die Krawatte aus, die Zigarre im Mund.

BABETTE: Warum ziehst du die Krawatte aus, Gottlieb?
Er übergibt ihr die Krawatte.

BIEDERMANN: Wenn ich sie anzeige, die beiden Gesellen, dann weiß ich, daß ich sie zu meinen Feinden mache. Was hast du davon!* Ein Streichholz genügt, und unser Haus steht in Flammen. Was hast du davon? Wenn ich hinaufgehe und sie einlade - sofern sie meine Einladung annehmen . . .

BABETTE: Dann?

BIEDERMANN: Sind wir eben Freunde. -
Er zieht seine Jacke aus, übergibt sie seiner Frau und geht.

BABETTE: Damit Sie's wissen, Anna: Sie haben dann heute abend keinen Ausgang. Wir haben Gesellschaft. Sie decken den Tisch für vier Personen.

Dachboden
Eisenring singt Lili Marlen, dann klopft es an die Tür.

EISENRING: Herein!
Er pfeift weiter, aber niemand tritt ein.
Herein!
Eintritt Biedermann, hemdärmelig, die Zigarre in der Hand.

EISENRING: Morgen, Herr Biedermann!

BIEDERMANN: Sie gestatten?

EISENRING: Wie haben Sie geschlafen?

BIEDERMANN: Danke, miserabel.

EISENRING: Ich auch. Wir haben Föhn . . .*
Er arbeitet weiter mit Schnur und Haspel.

BIEDERMANN: Ich möchte nicht stören.

EISENRING: Aber bitte, Herr Biedermann, Sie sind hier zu Haus.

BIEDERMANN: Ich möchte mich nicht aufdrängen . . .
Man hört Gurren der Tauben.
Wo ist denn unser Freund?

EISENRING: Der Sepp? An der Arbeit, der faule Hund. Wollte nicht gehen ohne Frühstück! Ich hab ihn geschickt, um Holzwolle aufzutreiben.

BIEDERMANN: Holzwolle – ?

EISENRING: Holzwolle trägt die Funken am weitesten.
Biedermann lacht höflich wie über einen schwachen Witz.

BIEDERMANN: Was ich habe sagen wollen, Herr Eisenring –

EISENRING: Sie wollen uns wieder hinausschmeißen?

BIEDERMANN: Mitten in der Nacht (meine Schlafpillen sind alle) ist es mir eingefallen: Sie haben ja hier oben, meine Herren, gar keine Toilette –

EISENRING: Wir haben die Dachrinne.

BIEDERMANN: Wie Sie wollen, meine Herren, wie Sie wollen.

Es ging mir nur so durch den Kopf. Die ganze Nacht. Vielleicht möchten Sie sich waschen oder duschen. Benutzen Sie getrost mein Badzimmer!* Ich habe Anna gesagt, sie soll Handtücher hinlegen.

Eisenring schüttelt den Kopf.

Warum schütteln Sie den Kopf?

EISENRING: Wo hat er sie jetzt wieder hingelegt?

BIEDERMANN: Was?

EISENRING: Haben Sie irgendwo eine Zündkapsel gesehen?

Er sucht da und dort.

Machen Sie sich keine Sorge, Herr Biedermann, wegen Badzimmer. Im Ernst. Im Gefängnis, wissen Sie, gab's auch kein Badzimmer.

BIEDERMANN: Gefängnis?

EISENRING: Hat Ihnen denn der Sepp nicht erzählt, daß ich aus dem Gefängnis komme?

BIEDERMANN: Nein.

EISENRING: Kein Wort?

BIEDERMANN: Nein.

EISENRING: Der erzählt alleweil nur von sich selbst. Gibt solche Leute! Schließlich was können wir dafür,* daß er so eine tragische Jugend gehabt hat. Haben Sie, Herr Biedermann, eine tragische Jugend gehabt? Ich nicht! – ich hätte studieren können, Papa wollte, daß ich Jurist werde.

Er steht an der Lukarne und unterhält sich mit den Tauben.

Grrr! Grrr! Grrr!

Biedermann zündet wieder seine Zigarre an.

BIEDERMANN: Herr Eisenring, ich habe die ganze Nacht nicht geschlafen, offen gesprochen: – ist wirklich Benzin in diesen Fässern?

EISENRING: Sie trauen uns nicht?

BIEDERMANN: Ich frag ja nur.

EISENRING: Wofür halten Sie uns, Herr Biedermann, offen gesprochen: wofür eigentlich?

BIEDERMANN: Sie müssen nicht denken, mein Freund, daß ich keinen Humor habe*, aber ihr habt eine Art zu scherzen, ich muß schon sagen. –

EISENRING: Wir lernen das.

BIEDERMANN: Was?

EISENRING: Scherz ist die drittbeste Tarnung. Die zweitbeste: Sentimentalität. Was unser Sepp so erzählt: Kindheit bei Köhlern im Wald, Waisenhaus, Zirkus und so. Aber die beste und sicherste Tarnung (finde ich) ist immer noch die blanke und nackte Wahrheit. Komischerweise. Die glaubt niemand.

Stube

Anna führt die schwarze Witwe Knechtling herein.*

ANNA: Nehmen Sie Platz!

Die Witwe setzt sich.

Aber wenn Sie die Frau Knechtling sind, dann hat's keinen Zweck, Herr Biedermann möchte nichts mit Ihnen zu tun haben, hat er gesagt –

Die Witwe erhebt sich.

Nehmen Sie Platz!

Die Witwe setzt sich.

Aber machen Sie sich keine Hoffnung . . .

Anna geht hinaus.

Dachboden

Eisenring steht und hantiert, Biedermann steht und raucht.

EISENRING: Wo unser Sepp nur so lange bleibt! Holzwolle ist doch keine Sache.* Hoffentlich haben sie ihn nicht geschnappt.

BIEDERMANN: Geschnappt?

EISENRING: Warum belustigt Sie das?

BIEDERMANN: Wenn Sie so reden, wissen Sie, Herr Eisenring,

Sie kommen für mich wie aus einer anderen Welt. Geschnappt! Ich finde es ja faszinierend. Wie aus einer andern Welt! In unseren Kreisen, wissen Sie, wird selten jemand geschnappt -

EISENRING: Weil man in Ihren Kreisen keine Holzwolle stiehlt, das ist klar, Herr Biedermann, das ist der Klassenunterschied.

BIEDERMANN: Unsinn!

EISENRING: Sie wollen doch nicht sagen. Herr Biedermann -

BIEDERMANN: Ich glaube nicht an Klassenunterschiede! - das müssen Sie doch gespürt haben, Eisenring, ich bin nicht altmodisch. Im Gegenteil. Ich bedaure es aufrichtig, daß man gerade in den unteren Klassen immer noch von Klassenunterschied schwatzt. Sind wir denn heutzutage nicht alle, ob arm oder reich, Geschöpfe eines gleichen Schöpfers? Auch der Mittelstand. Sind wir, Sie und ich, nicht Menschen aus Fleisch und Blut? . . . Ich weiß nicht, mein Herr, ob Sie auch Zigarren rauchen?
Er bietet an, aber Eisenring schüttelt den Kopf.
Ich rede nicht für Gleichmacherei,* versteht sich, es wird immer Tüchtige und Untüchtige geben, Gott sei Dank, aber warum reichen wir uns nicht einfach die Hände? Ein bißchen guten Willen, Herrgottnochmal, ein bißchen Idealismus, ein bißchen - und wir alle hätten unsere Ruhe und unseren Frieden, die Armen und die Reichen, meinen Sie nicht?

EISENRING: Wenn ich offen sein darf, Herr Biedermann: -

BIEDERMANN: Ich bitte drum.

EISENRING: Nehmen Sie's nicht krumm?

BIEDERMANN: Je offener, um so besser.

EISENRING: Ich meine: - offen gesprochen: - Sie sollten hier nicht rauchen.
Biedermann erschrickt und löscht die Zigarre.

Ich habe Ihnen hier keine Vorschriften zu machen, Herr Biedermann, schließlich und endlich ist es Ihr eigenes Haus, aber Sie verstehen –

BIEDERMANN: Selbstverständlich!

Eisenring bückt sich.

EISENRING: Da liegt sie ja!

Er nimmt etwas vom Boden und bläst es sauber, bevor er es an der Schnur befestigt, neuerdings pfeifend: Lili Marlen.

BIEDERMANN: Sagen Sie, Herr Eisenring: Was machen Sie eigentlich die ganze Zeit? Wenn ich fragen darf. Was ist das eigentlich?

EISENRING: Die Zündkapsel.

BIEDERMANN: – ?

EISENRING: Und das ist die Zündschnur.

BIEDERMANN: – ?

EISENRING: Es soll jetzt noch bessere geben, sagt der Sepp, neuerdings. Aber die haben sie noch nicht in den Zeughäusern, und kaufen kommt für uns ja nicht in Frage. Alles was mit Krieg zu tun hat, ist furchtbar teuer, immer nur erste Qualität.

BIEDERMANN: Zündschnur? sagen Sie.

EISENRING: Knallzündschnur.

Er gibt Biedermann das Ende der Schnur.

Wenn Sie so freundlich sein möchten, Herr Biedermann, dieses Ende zu halten, damit ich messen kann.

Biedermann hält die Schnur.

BIEDERMANN: Spaß beiseite, mein Freund –

EISENRING: Nur einen Augenblick!

Er pfeift Lili Marlen und mißt die Zündschnur.

Danke, Herr Biedermann, danke sehr!

Biedermann muß plötzlich lachen.

BIEDERMANN: Nein, Willi, mich können Sie nicht ins Bockshorn jagen. Mich nicht! Aber ich muß schon sagen,

Sie verlassen sich sehr auf den Humor der Leute. Sehr! Wenn Sie so reden, kann ich mir schon vorstellen, daß man Sie ab und zu verhaftet. Nicht alle, mein Freund, nicht alle haben soviel Humor wie ich!

EISENRING: Man muß die Richtigen finden.

BIEDERMANN: An meinem Stammtisch zum Beispiel, die sehen schon Sodom und Gomorra,* wenn man nur sagt, man glaube an das Gute in den Menschen.

EISENRING: Ha.

BIEDERMANN: Und dabei habe ich unsrer Feuerwehr eine Summe gestiftet, die ich gar nicht nennen will.

EISENRING: Ha.
Er legt die Zündschnur aus.
Die Leute, die keinen Humor haben, sind genau so verloren, wenn's losgeht; seien Sie getrost!*
Biedermann muß sich auf ein Faß setzen, Schweiß.
Was ist denn? Herr Biedermann? Sie sind ja ganz bleich!
Er klopft ihm auf die Schulter.
Das ist dieser Geruch, ich weiß, wenn's einer nicht gewohnt ist, dieser Benzingeruch, ich werde noch ein Fensterchen öffnen – *Eisenring öffnet die Tür.*

BIEDERMANN: Danke . . .
Anna ruft im Treppenhaus.

ANNA: Herr Biedermann! Herr Biedermann!

EISENRING: Schon wieder die Polizei?

ANNA: Herr Biedermann!

EISENRING: Wenn das kein Polizeistaat ist.*

ANNA: Herr Biedermann!

BIEDERMANN: Ich komme!
Es wird nur noch geflüstert.
Herr Eisenring, mögen Sie Gans?

EISENRING: Gans?

BIEDERMANN: Gans, ja, Gans.

EISENRING: Mögen? Ich? Wieso?

BIEDERMANN: Gefüllt mit Kastanien.

EISENRING: Und Rotkraut dazu?

BIEDERMANN: Ja . . . Was ich nämlich habe sagen wollen: Meine Frau und ich, vor allem ich – ich dachte nur: Wenn es Ihnen Freude macht . . . Ich will mich nicht aufdrängen! – wenn es Ihnen Freude macht, Herr Eisenring, zu einem netten Abendessen zu kommen, Sie und der Sepp –

EISENRING: Heute?

BIEDERMANN: Oder lieber morgen?

EISENRING: Morgen, glaub ich, sind wir nicht mehr da. Aber heute mit Vergnügen, Herr Biedermann, mit Vergnügen!

BIEDERMANN: Sagen wir: Sieben Uhr.

Anna ruft im Treppenhaus.

ANNA: Herr Biedermann –

Er gibt die Hand.

BIEDERMANN: Abgemacht?

EISENRING: Abgemacht.

Biedermann geht und bleibt in der Türe nochmals stehen, freundlich nickend, während er einen stieren Blick auf Fässer und Zündschnur wirft.

EISENRING: Abgemacht.

Biedermann geht, und Eisenring arbeitet weiter, indem er pfeift. Vortritt der Chor, als wäre die Szene zu Ende; aber im Augenblick, wo der Chor sich an der Rampe versammelt hat, gibt es Lärm auf dem Dachboden; irgend etwas ist umgefallen.

Dachboden

EISENRING: Du kannst rauskommen, Doktor.

Ein Dritter kriecht zwischen den Fässern hervor, Brillenträger.

Du hast's gehört: Wir müssen zu einem Nachtessen, der

Sepp und ich, du machst die Wache hier. Daß keiner hereinkommt und raucht. Verstanden? Bevor's Zeit ist.

Der Dritte putzt seine Brille.

Ich frag mich manchmal, Doktor, was du eigentlich machst bei uns, wenn du keine Freude hast an Feuersbrünsten, an Funken und prasselnden Flammen, an Sirenen, die immer zu spät sind, an Hundegebell und Rauch und Menschengeschrei – und Asche.

Der Dritte setzt seine Brille auf; stumm und ernst. Eisenring lacht.

Weltverbesserer!

Er pfeift eine kurze Weile vor sich hin, ohne den Doktor anzusehen.

Ich mag euch Akademiker nicht, aber das weißt du, Doktor, das sagte ich dir sofort: 's ist keine rechte Freude dabei, euresgleichen ist immer so ideologisch, immer so ernst, bis es reicht zum Verrat* – 's ist keine rechte Freude dabei.

Er hantiert weiter und pfeift weiter.

Chor

Wir sind bereit.
Sorgsam gerollt sind die Schläuche, die roten,
Alles laut Vorschrift,
Blank ist und sorgsam geschmiert und aus Messing
Jeglicher Haspel.
Jedermann weiß, was zu tun ist.

CHORFÜHRER: Leider herrscht Föhn –

CHOR: Jedermann weiß, was zu tun ist,
Blank auch und sorgsam geprüft,
Daß es an Druck uns nicht fehle,
Ist unsere Pumpe,
Gleichfalls aus Messing.

CHORFÜHRER: Und die Hydranten?

CHOR: Jedermann weiß, was zu tun ist,

CHORFÜHRER: Wir sind bereit. –

Es kommen Babette, eine Gans in der Hand, und der Dr. phil.

BABETTE: Ja, Herr Doktor, ja, ich weiß, aber mein Mann, ja, es ist dringend, Herr Doktor, es ist dringend, ja, ich werde es ihm sagen –
Sie läßt den Doktor stehen und tritt an die Rampe.
Mein Mann hat eine Gans bestellt, bitte, da ist sie. Und ich soll sie braten!
Damit wir Freunde werden mit denen da oben.
Man hört Kirchenglockengeläute. *
Es ist Samstagabend, wie Sie hören, und ich werde so eine dumme Ahnung nicht los: daß sie vielleicht zum letzten Mal so läuten, die Glocken unsrer Stadt . . .
Biedermann ruft nach Babette.
Ich weiß nicht, meine Damen, ob Gottlieb immer recht hat. Das hat er nämlich schon einmal gesagt: Natürlich sind's Halunken, aber wenn ich sie zu meinen Feinden mache, Babette, dann ist unser Haarwasser hin!* Und kaum war er in der Partei* – *Biedermann ruft nach Babette.*
Immer das gleiche! Ich kenne meinen Gottlieb. Immer wieder ist er zu gutmütig, ach, einfach zu gutmütig!
Babette geht mit der Gans.

CHOR: Einer mit Brille.
Sohn wohl aus besserem Haus,
Neidlos,
Aber belesen, so scheint mir, und bleich,
Nimmermehr hoffend, es komme das Gute
Aus Gutmütigkeit,
Sondern entschlossen zu jedweder Tat,
Nämlich es heiligt die Mittel (so hofft er) der Zweck,*
Ach,
Hoffend auch er . . . bieder-unbieder!*
Putzend die Brille, um Weitsicht zu haben,
Sieht er in Fässern voll Brennstoff
Nicht Brennstoff –
Er nämlich sieht die Idee!
Bis es brennt.

DR. PHIL: Guten Abend . . .

CHORFÜHRER: An die Schläuche!
An die Pumpe!
An die Leiter!
Die Feuerwehrmänner rennen an ihre Plätze.

CHORFÜHRER: Guten Abend.
Zum Publikum; nachdem man Bereit-Rufe von überall gehört hat.
Wir sind bereit. –

SZENE 5

Stube
Die Witwe Knechtling ist noch immer da, sie steht. Man hört das Glockengeläute sehr laut. Anna deckt den Tisch, und Biedermann bringt zwei Sessel.

BIEDERMANN: – weil ich, wie Sie sehen, keine Zeit habe, Frau Knechtling, keine Zeit, um mich mit Toten zu befassen – wie gesagt: Wenden Sie sich an meinen Rechtsanwalt.
Die Witwe Knechtling geht.
Man hört ja seine eigne Stimme nicht, Anna, machen Sie das Fenster zu!
Anna macht das Fenster zu, und das Geläute tönt leiser.
Ich habe gesagt: Ein schlichtes und gemütliches Abendessen.
Was sollen diese idiotischen Kandelaber!

ANNA: Haben wir aber immer, Herr Biedermann.

BIEDERMANN: Schlicht und gemütlich, sag ich. Nur keine Protzerei! – und diese Wasserschalen, verdammtnochmal! diese Messerbänklein, Silber, nichts als Silber und Kristall. Was macht das für einen Eindruck!
Er sammelt die Messerbänklein und steckt sie in die Hosentasche.
Sie sehen doch, Anna, ich trage meine älteste Hausjacke, und Sie – Das große Geflügelmesser können Sie lassen,

Anna, das brauchen wir. Aber sonst: Weg mit diesem Silber! Die beiden Herren sollen sich wie zu Haus fühlen . . . Wo ist der Korkenzieher?

ANNA: Hier.

BIEDERMANN: Haben wir nichts Einfacheres?

ANNA: In der Küche, aber der ist rostig.

BIEDERMANN: Her damit!

Er nimmt einen Silberkübel vom Tisch.

Was soll denn das?

ANNA: Für den Wein –

BIEDERMANN: Silber!

Er starrt auf den Kübel und dann auf Anna.

Haben wir das immer?

ANNA: Das braucht man doch, Herr Biedermann.

BIEDERMANN: Brauchen! Was heißt brauchen? Was wir brauchen, das ist Menschlichkeit, Brüderlichkeit. Weg damit! – und was, zum Teufel, bringen Sie denn da?

ANNA: Servietten.

BIEDERMANN: Damast!

ANNA: Wir haben keine andern.

Er sammelt die Servietten und steckt sie in den Silberkübel.

BIEDERMANN: Es gibt ganze Völkerstämme, die ohne Servietten leben, Menschen wie wir –

Eintritt Babette mit einem großen Kranz, Biedermann bemerkt sie noch nicht, er steht vor dem Tisch.

Ich frage mich, wozu wir überhaupt ein Tischtuch brauchen –

BABETTE: Gottlieb?

BIEDERMANN: Nur keine Klassenunterschiede!

Er sieht Babette.

Was soll dieser Kranz?

BABETTE: Den wir bestellt haben. Was sagst du dazu, Gottlieb, jetzt schicken sie den Kranz hierher. Dabei habe ich ihnen selber die Adresse geschrieben, die Adresse von Knechtlings, schwarz auf weiß. Und die Schleife und alles ist verkehrt!

BIEDERMANN: Die Schleife, wieso?

BABETTE: Und die Rechnung, sagt der Bursche, die haben sie an die Frau Knechtling geschickt.
Sie zeigt die Schleife.
UNSEREM UNVERGESSLICHEN GOTTLIEB BIEDERMANN
Er betrachtet die Schleife.

BIEDERMANN: Das nehmen wir nicht an. Kommt nicht in Frage! Das müssen sie ändern –
Er geht zum Tisch zurück.
Mach mich jetzt nicht nervös, Babette, ich habe anderes zu tun, Herrgottnochmal, ich kann nicht überall sein.
Babette geht mit dem Kranz.
Also weg mit dem Tischtuch! Helfen Sie mir doch, Anna. Und wie gesagt: Es wird nicht serviert. Unter keinen Umständen! Sie kommen herein, ohne zu klopfen, einfach herein und stellen die Pfanne einfach auf den Tisch –

ANNA: Die Pfanne?
Er nimmt das Tischtuch weg.

BIEDERMANN: Sofort eine ganz andere Stimmung. Sehn Sie! Ein hölzerner Tisch, nichts weiter, wie beim Abendmahl.*
Er gibt ihr das Tischtuch.

ANNA: Herr Biedermann meinen, ich soll die Gans einfach in der Pfanne bringen?
Sie faltet das Tischtuch zusammen.
Was für einen Wein, Herr Biedermann, soll ich denn holen?

BIEDERMANN: Ich hole ihn selbst.

ANNA: Herr Biedermann!

BIEDERMANN: Was denn noch?

ANNA: Ich hab aber keinen solchen Pullover, wie Sie sagen, Herr Biedermann, so einen schlichten, daß man meint, ich gehöre zur Familie.

BIEDERMANN: Nehmen Sie's bei meiner Frau!

ANNA: Den gelben oder den roten?

BIEDERMANN: Nur keine Umstände! Ich will kein Häubchen sehen und kein Schürzchen. Verstanden? Und wie gesagt: Weg mit diesen Kandelabern! Und überhaupt: Sehen Sie zu, Anna, daß hier nicht alles so ordentlich ist!
. . . Ich bin im Keller.
Biedermann geht hinaus.

ANNA: »Sehen Sie zu, daß hier nicht alles so ordentlich ist!«
Sie schleudert das Tischtuch, nachdem es zusammengefaltet ist, in irgendeine Ecke und tritt mit beiden Füßen drauf.
Bitte sehr.*
Eintreten Schmitz und Eisenring, jeder mit einer Rose in der Hand.*

BEIDE: Guten Abend, Fräulein!
Anna geht hinaus, ohne die beiden anzublicken.

EISENRING: Wieso keine Holzwolle?

SCHMITZ: Beschlagnahmt. Polizeilich. Vorsichtsmaßnahme. Wer Holzwolle verkauft oder besitzt, ohne eine polizeiliche Genehmigung zu haben, wird verhaftet. Vorsichtsmaßnahme im ganzen Land . . .
Er kämmt sich die Haare.

EISENRING: Hast du noch Streichhölzchen?

SCHMITZ: Ich nicht.

EISENRING: Ich auch nicht.
Schmitz bläst seinen Kamm aus.

SCHMITZ: Müssen ihn darum bitten.

EISENRING: Biedermann?

SCHMITZ: Aber nicht vergessen.
Er steckt den Kamm ein und schnuppert.
Mh, wie das schon duftet . . .
Biedermann tritt an die Rampe, Flaschen im Arm.

BIEDERMANN: Sie können über mich denken, meine Herren, wie Sie wollen. Aber antworten Sie mir auf eine Frage: –
Man hört Grölen und Lachen.
Ich sag mir: Solange sie grölen und saufen, tun sie nichts anderes . . . Die besten Flaschen aus meinem Keller, hätte es mir einer vor einer Woche gesagt – Hand aufs Herz: Seit wann (genau) wissen Sie, meine Herren, daß es Brandstifter sind? Es kommt eben nicht so, meine Herren, wie Sie meinen – sondern langsam und plötzlich . . . Verdacht! Das hatte ich sofort, meine Herren, Verdacht hat man immer – aber Hand aufs Herz, meine Herren: Was hätten Sie denn getan, Herrgottnochmal, an meiner Stelle? Und wann?
Er horcht, und es ist still.
Ich muß hinauf!
Er entfernt sich geschwind.

SZENE 6

Stube
Das Gansessen ist im vollen Gang, Gelächter, vor allem Biedermann (noch mit den Flaschen im Arm) kann sich von dem Witz, der gefallen ist, nicht mehr erholen; nur Babette lacht durchaus nicht.*

BIEDERMANN: Putzfäden! Hast du das wieder gehört? Putzfäden, sagt er, Putzfäden brennen noch besser!

BABETTE: Wieso ist das ein Witz?

BIEDERMANN: Putzfäden! – Weißt du, was Putzfäden sind?

BABETTE: Ja.

BIEDERMANN: Du hast keinen Humor, Babettchen.
Er stellt die Flasche auf den Tisch.
Was soll man machen, meine Freunde, wenn jemand einfach keinen Humor hat?

BABETTE: So erkläre es mir doch.

BIEDERMANN: Also! – heute morgen sagt der Willi, er hätte den Sepp geschickt, um Holzwolle zu stehlen. Holzwolle, das verstehst du? Und jetzt frage ich den Sepp: Was macht denn die Holzwolle?* worauf er sagt: Holzwolle habe er nicht auftreiben können, aber Putzfäden. Verstehst du? Und Willi sagt: Putzfäden brennen noch viel besser!

BABETTE: Das habe ich verstanden.

BIEDERMANN: Ja? Hast du verstanden?

BABETTE: Und was ist der Witz dran?*

Biedermann gibt es auf.

BIEDERMANN: Trinken wir, meine Herren!

Biedermann entkorkt die Flasche.

BABETTE: Ist das denn wahr, Herr Schmitz, Sie haben Putzfäden auf unseren Dachboden gebracht?

BIEDERMANN: Du wirst lachen, Babette, heute vormittag haben wir zusammen sogar die Zündschnur gemessen, der Willi und ich.

BABETTE: Zündschnur?

BIEDERMANN: Knallzündschnur!

Er füllt die Gläser.

BABETTE: Jetzt aber im Ernst, meine Herren, was soll das alles?

Biedermann lacht.

BIEDERMANN: Im Ernst! sagt sie. Im Ernst! Hören Sie das? Im Ernst! . . . Laß dich nicht foppen, Babette, ich hab's dir gesagt, unsere Freunde haben eine Art zu scherzen – andere Kreise, andere Witze!* sag ich immer . . . Es fehlt jetzt nur noch, daß sie mich um Streichhölzchen bitten!

Schmitz und Eisenring geben einander einen Blick.

Nämlich die beiden Herren halten mich immer noch für einen ängstlichen Spießer, der keinen Humor hat, weißt du, den man ins Bockshorn jagen kann* – *Er hebt sein Glas.* Prost!

EISENRING: Prost!

SCHMITZ: Prost!

Sie stoßen an.

BIEDERMANN: Auf unsere Freundschaft.

Sie trinken und setzen sich wieder.

In unserem Haus wird nicht serviert, meine Herren, Sie greifen einfach zu.

SCHMITZ: Aber ich kann nicht mehr.

EISENRING: Zier dich nicht. Du bist nicht im Waisenhaus, Sepp, zier dich nicht.

Er bedient sich mit Gans.

Ihre Gans, Madame, ist Klasse.*

BABETTE: Das freut mich.

EISENRING: Gans und Pommard!* – dazu gehörte eigentlich bloß noch ein Tischtuch.

BABETTE: Hörst du's Gottlieb?

EISENRING: Es muß aber nicht sein!* – so ein weißes Tischtuch, wissen Sie, Damast mit Silber drauf.

BIEDERMANN: Anna!

EISENRING: Damast mit Blumen drin, aber weiß, wissen Sie, wie Eisblumen! – es muß aber nicht sein, Herr Biedermann, es muß aber nicht sein. Im Gefängnis haben wir auch kein Tischtuch gehabt.

BIEDERMANN: Anna!

BABETTE: Im Gefängnis – ?

BIEDERMANN: Wo ist sie denn?

BABETTE: Sie sind im Gefängnis gewesen?

Anna kommt; sie trägt einen knallroten Pullover.

BIEDERMANN: Anna, bringen Sie sofort ein Tischtuch!

ANNA: Sehr wohl. –

EISENRING: Und wenn Sie so etwas wie Fingerschalen haben –

ANNA: Sehr wohl. –

EISENRING: Sie finden es vielleicht kindisch, Madame,

aber so sind halt die Leute aus dem Volk.* Sepp zum Beispiel, der bei den Köhlern aufgewachsen ist und noch nie ein Messerbänklein gesehen hat, sehen Sie, es ist nun einmal der Traum seines verpfuschten Lebens: – so eine Tafel mit Silber und Kristall!

BABETTE: Gottlieb, das haben wir doch alles.

EISENRING: Aber es muß nicht sein.

ANNA: Bitte sehr.

EISENRING: Und wenn Sie schon Servietten haben, Fräulein: Her damit!

ANNA: Herr Biedermann hat gesagt –

BIEDERMANN: Her damit!

ANNA: Bitte sehr.

Ann bringt alles wieder herbei.

EISENRING: Sie nehmen es hoffentlich nicht krumm, Madame. Wenn man aus dem Gefängnis kommt, wissen Sie, monatelang ohne Kultur –

Er nimmt das Tischtuch und zeigt es Schmitz.

Weißt du, was das ist?

Hinüber zu Babette.

Hat er noch nie gesehen!

Wieder zurück zu Schmitz.

Das ist Damast.

SCHMITZ: Und jetzt? Was soll ich damit?

Eisenring bindet ihm das Tischtuch um den Hals.

EISENRING: So. –

Biedermann versucht, es lustig zu finden und lacht.

BABETTE: Und wo sind denn unsere Messerbänklein, Anna, unsere Messerbänklein?

ANNA: Herr Biedermann –

BIEDERMANN: Her damit!

ANNA: Sie haben gesagt: Weg damit.

BIEDERMANN: Her damit! sag ich. Wo sind sie denn, Herrgottnochmal?

ANNA: In Ihrer linken Hosentasche.

Biedermann greift in die Hosentasche und findet sie.

EISENRING: Nur keine Aufregung.

ANNA: Ich kann doch nichts dafür!*

EISENRING: Nur keine Aufregung, Fräulein –

Anna bricht in Heulen aus, dreht sich und läuft weg.

EISENRING: Das ist der Föhn.

Pause

BIEDERMANN: Trinken Sie, meine Freunde, trinken Sie!

Sie trinken und schweigen.

EISENRING: Gans habe ich jeden Tag gegessen, wissen Sie, als Kellner. Wenn man so durch die langen Korridore flitzt, die Platte auf der flachen Hand. Aber dann, Madame, wo putzt unsereiner die Finger ab? Das ist es.* Wo anders als an den eignen Haaren? – während andere Menschen eine kristallene Wasserschale dafür haben! Das ist's, was ich nie vergessen werde. *Er taucht seine Finger in die Fingerschale.*
Wissen Sie, was ein Trauma ist?

BIEDERMANN: Nein.

EISENRING: Haben sie mir im Gefängnis alles erklärt . . .

Er trocknet seine Finger ab.

BABETTE: Und wieso, Herr Eisenring, sind Sie denn ins Gefängnis gekommen?

BIEDERMANN: Babette!

EISENRING: Wieso ich ins Gefängnis gekommen bin?

BIEDERMANN: Das fragt man doch nicht!

EISENRING: Ich frage mich selbst . . . Ich war ein Kellner, wie gesagt, ein kleiner Oberkellner, und plötzlich verwechselten sie mich mit einem großen Brandstifter.

BIEDERMANN: Hm.

EISENRING: Verhafteten mich in meiner Wohnung.

BIEDERMANN: Hm.

EISENRING: Ich war so erstaunt, daß ich drauf einging.

BIEDERMANN: Hm.

EISENRING: Ich hatte Glück, Madame, ich hatte sieben ausgesprochen reizende Polizisten. Als ich sagte, ich müsse an meine Arbeit und hätte keine Zeit, sagten sie: Ihr Etablissement ist niedergebrannt.

BIEDERMANN: Niedergebrannt?

EISENRING: So über Nacht, scheint es, ja.

BABETTE: Niedergebrannt?

EISENRING: Schön! sagte ich: Dann hab ich Zeit. Es war nur noch ein rauchendes Gebälk, unser Etablissement, ich sah es im Vorbeifahren, wissen Sie, durch dieses kleine Gitterfenster aus dem Gefängniswagen.
Er trinkt kennerhaft.

BIEDERMANN: Und dann?
Eisenring betrachtet die Etikette.

EISENRING: Den hatten wir auch: Neunundvierziger! Cave de l'Echannon . . .* Und dann? Das muß Ihnen der Sepp erzählen. Als ich so im Vorzimmer sitze und mit den Handschellen spiele, sage und schreibe, wer wird da hereingeführt? – der da!
Schmitz strahlt.
Prost, Sepp!

SCHMITZ: Prost, Willi!
Sie trinken.

BIEDERMANN: Und dann?

SCHMITZ: Sind Sie der Brandstifter? fragt man ihn und bietet Zigaretten an. Entschuldigen Sie! sagt er. Streichhölzchen habe ich leider nicht, Herr Kommissar, obschon Sie mich für einen Brandstifter halten –
Sie lachen dröhnend und hauen sich auf die Schenkel.

BIEDERMANN: Hm. –

Anna ist eingetreten, sie trägt wieder Häubchen und Schürzchen, sie überreicht eine Visitenkarte, die Biedermann sich ansieht.

ANNA: Es ist dringend, sagt er.

BIEDERMANN: Wenn ich aber Gäste habe –

Schmitz und Eisenring stoßen wieder an.

SCHMITZ: Prost, Willi!

EISENRING: Prost, Sepp!

Sie trinken, Biedermann betrachtet die Visitenkarte.

BABETTE: Wer ist es denn, Gottlieb?

BIEDERMANN: Dieser Dr. phil . . .

Anna betätigt sich beim Schrank.

EISENRING: Und was ist denn das andere dort, Fräulein, das Silberne dort?

ANNA: Die Kandelaber?

EISENRING: Warum verstecken Sie das?

BIEDERMANN: Her damit!

ANNA: Herr Biedermann haben selbst gesagt –

BIEDERMANN: Her damit! sag ich.

Anna stellt die Kandelaber auf den Tisch.

EISENRING: Sepp, was sagst du dazu? Haben sie Kandelaber und verstecken sie!* Was willst du noch? Silber mit Kerzen drauf . . . Hast Du Streichhölzer?

Er greift in seine Hosentasche.

SCHMITZ: Ich? Nein.

Er greift in seine Hosentasche.

EISENRING: Leider haben wir gar keine Streichhölzer, Herr Biedermann, tatsächlich.

BIEDERMANN: Ich habe.

EISENRING: Geben Sie her!

BIEDERMANN: Ich mach es schon. Lassen Sie nur. Ich mach es schon.
Er zündet die Kerzen an.

BABETTE: Was will denn der Herr?

ANNA: Ich versteh ihn nicht, Madame, er kann nicht länger schweigen, sagt er und wartet im Treppenhaus.

BABETTE: Unter vier Augen? sagt er.

ANNA: Ja, und dann will er immer etwas enthüllen.

BABETTE: Was?

ANNA: Das versteh ich nicht, Madame, und wenn er's mir hundertmal sagt;* er sagt: er möchte sich distanzieren . . .
Es leuchten viele Kerzen.

EISENRING: Macht doch sofort einen ganz anderen Eindruck, finden Sie nicht, Madame? Candlelight.

BABETTE: Ach ja.

EISENRING: Ich bin für Stimmung.

BIEDERMANN: Sehen Sie, Herr Eisenring, das freut mich . . .
Es sind alle Kerzen angezündet.

EISENRING: Schmitz, schmatze nicht!
Babette nimmt Eisenring zur Seite.

BABETTE: Lassen Sie ihn doch!

EISENRING: Er hat kein Benehmen, Madame, ich bitte um Entschuldigung; es ist mir furchtbar. Woher soll er's haben! Von der Köhlerhütte zum Waisenhaus –

BABETTE: Ich weiß!

EISENRING: Vom Waisenhaus zum Zirkus –

BABETTE: Ich weiß!

EISENRING: Vom Zirkus zum Theater.

BABETTE: Das habe ich nicht gewußt, nein –

EISENRING: Schicksale, Madame, Schicksale!
Babette wendet sich an Schmitz.

BABETTE: Beim Theater sind Sie auch gewesen?

Schmitz nagt ein Gansbein und nickt.
Wo denn?

SCHMITZ: Hinten.

EISENRING: Dabei ist er begabt* – Sepp als Geist, haben Sie das schon erlebt?

SCHMITZ: Aber nicht jetzt!

EISENRING: Wieso nicht?

SCHMITZ: Ich war nur eine Woche beim Theater, Madame, dann ist es niedergebrannt –

BABETTE: Niedergebrannt?

EISENRING: Zier dich nicht!

BIEDERMANN: Niedergebrannt?

EISENRING: Zier dich nicht!
Er löst das Tischtuch, das Schmitz als Serviette getragen hat, und wirft es dem Schmitz über den Kopf.
Los!
Schmitz, verhüllt mit dem weißen Tischtuch, erhebt sich.
Bitte. Sieht er nicht aus wie ein Geist?

ANNA: Ich hab aber Angst.

EISENRING: Mädelchen!
Er nimmt Anna in seinen Arm, sie hält die Hände vors Gesicht.

SCHMITZ: »Können wir?«

EISENRING: Das ist Theatersprache, Madame, das hat er auf den Proben gelernt in einer einzigen Woche, bevor es niedergebrannt ist, erstaunlicherweise.

BABETTE: Reden Sie doch nicht immer von Bränden!

SCHMITZ: »Können wir?«

EISENRING: Bereit. –
Alle sitzen, Eisenring hält Anna an seiner Brust.

SCHMITZ: JEDERMANN! JEDERMANN!*

BABETTE: Gottlieb –?

BIEDERMANN: Still!

BABETTE: Das haben wir in Salzburg gesehen.

SCHMITZ: BIEDERMANN! BIEDERMANN!

EISENRING: Ich find's großartig, wie er das macht.

SCHMITZ: BIEDERMANN! BIEDERMANN!

EISENRING: Sie müssen fragen, wer bist du?

BIEDERMANN: Ich?

EISENRING: Sonst wird er seinen Text nicht los.*

SCHMITZ: JEDERMANN! BIEDERMANN!

BIEDERMANN: Also: – wer bin ich?

BABETTE: Nein! Du mußt doch fragen, wer er ist.

BIEDERMANN: Ah so.

SCHMITZ: HÖRT IHR MICH NICHT?

EISENRING: Nein, Sepp, nochmals von Anfang an!
Sie nehmen eine andere Stellung ein.

SCHMITZ: JEDERMANN! BIEDERMANN!

BABETTE: Bist du – zum Beispiel – der Tod?

BIEDERMANN: Quatsch!

BABETTE: Was kann er denn sonst sein?

BIEDERMANN: Du mußt fragen: Wer bist du? er kann auch der Geist von Hamlet* sein. Oder der Steinerne Gast, weißt du. Oder dieser Dingsda, wie heißt er schon: der Mitarbeiter von Macbeth . . .

SCHMITZ: WER RUFT MICH?

EISENRING: Weiter.

SCHMITZ: BIEDERMANN GOTTLIEB!

BABETTE: Frag du ihn doch, er spricht zu dir.

SCHMITZ: HÖRT IHR MICH NICHT?

BIEDERMANN: Wer bist du denn?

SCHMITZ: ICH BIN DER GEIST – VON KNECHTLING.
Babette springt auf und schreit.

EISENRING: Stop.
Er reißt dem Schmitz das weiße Tischtuch herunter.
Ein Idiot bist du! Das kannst du doch nicht machen. Knechtling! Der geht doch nicht. Knechtling ist heute begraben worden.

SCHMITZ: Eben.
Babette hält ihre Hände vors Gesicht.

EISENRING: Madame, er ist es nicht!
Er schüttelt den Kopf über Schmitz.
Wie kannst du so geschmacklos sein?

SCHMITZ: Es fiel mir nichts anderes ein . . .

EISENRING: Knechtling! Ausgerechnet. Ein alter und treuer Mitarbeiter von Herrn Biedermann, stell dir das vor: Heute begraben – der ist ja noch ganz beisammen, bleich wie ein Tischtuch, weißlich und glänzend wie Damast, steif und kalt, aber zum Hinstellen . . .*
Er faßt Babette an der Schulter.
Ehrenwort, Madame, er ist es nicht.
Schmitz wischt sich den Schweiß.

SCHMITZ: Entschuldigung.

BIEDERMANN: Setzen wir uns.

ANNA: Ist das jetzt alles?
Man setzt sich, Pause der Verlegenheit.

BIEDERMANN: Wie wär's mit einer kleinen Zigarre, meine Herren?
Er bietet eine Schachtel mit Zigarren an.

EISENRING: Idiot! da siehst du's, wie Herr Biedermann zittert . . . Danke, Herr Biedermann, danke! . . . Wenn du meinst, das sei lustig. Wo du genau weißt: Knechtling hat sich unter den Gasherd gelegt, nachdem unser Gottlieb getan hat, was er konnte, für diesen Knechtling. Vierzehn Jahre lang hat er ihm Arbeit gegeben, diesem Knechtling, das ist der Dank –

BIEDERMANN: Reden wir nicht mehr davon.

EISENRING: Das ist dein Dank für die Gans!
Sie rüsten ihre Zigarren.

SCHMITZ: Soll ich etwas singen?

EISENRING: Was?

SCHMITZ: »Fuchs, du hast die Gans gestohlen – «*
Er singt mit voller Stimme.
»Fuchs, du hast die Gans gestohlen, gib sie wieder her – «

EISENRING: Laß das.

SCHMITZ: »Gib sie wieder her,
Sonst wird dich der Jäger holen – «

EISENRING: Er ist betrunken.

SCHMITZ: »Mit dem Scheißgewehr.«*

EISENRING: Hören Sie nicht zu, Madame.

SCHMITZ: »Gib sie wieder her,
Sonst wird dich der Jäger holen
Mit dem Scheißgewehr!«

BIEDERMANN: Scheißgewehr ist gut.

ALLE MÄNNER :»Fuchs, du hast die Gans gestohlen – «
Sie singen mehrstimmig, einmal sehr laut, einmal sehr leise, Wechselgesang jeder Art, Gelächter und grölende Verbrüderung, einmal eine Pause, aber dann ist es Biedermann, der wieder anhebt und in der Spaßigkeit vorangeht, bis sich das Ganze erschöpft.

BIEDERMANN: Also: – Prost!
Sie heben die Gläser, und man hört Sirenen in der Ferne.
Was war das?

EISENRING: Sirenen.

BIEDERMANN: Spaß beiseite! –

BABETTE: Brandstifter, Brandstifter!

BIEDERMANN: Schrei nicht.
Babette reißt das Fenster auf, und die Sirenen kommen näher, heulen, daß es durch Mark und Bein geht, und sausen vorbei.

BIEDERMANN: Wenigstens nicht bei uns.

BABETTE: Wo kann das nur sein?

EISENRING: Wo der Föhn herkommt.

BIEDERMANN: Wenigstens nicht bei uns . . .

EISENRING: Das machen wir meistens so. Wir holen die Feuerwehr in ein billiges Außenviertel, und später, wenn's wirklich losgeht, ist ihnen der Rückweg versperrt.

BIEDERMANN: Nein, meine Herren, Spaß beiseite –

SCHMITZ: So machen wir's aber, Spaß beiseite.

BIEDERMANN: Schluß mit diesem Unsinn! ich bitte Sie. Alles mit Maß, Sie sehen, meine Frau ist kreidebleich.

BABETTE: Und du?!

BIEDERMANN: Und überhaupt: Sirenen sind Sirenen, darüber kann ich nicht lachen, meine Herren, irgendwo hört's auf, irgendwo brennt's, sonst würde unsere Feuerwehr nicht ausfahren.
Eisenring blickt auf seine Uhr.

EISENRING: Wir müssen gehen.

BIEDERMANN: Jetzt?

EISENRING: Leider.

SCHMITZ: »Sonst wird dich der Jäger holen . . .«
Man hört nochmals die Sirenen.

BIEDERMANN: Mach einen Kaffee, Babette!
Babette geht hinaus.
Und Sie, Anna, was* stehen Sie da und glotzen?
Anna geht hinaus.
Unter uns, meine Herren: Genug ist genug: Meine Frau ist herzkrank. Scherzen wir nicht länger über Brandstifterei.

SCHMITZ: Wir scherzen ja nicht, Herr Biedermann.

EISENRING: Wir sind Brandstifter.

BIEDERMANN: Meine Herren, jetzt ganz im Ernst –

SCHMITZ: Ganz im Ernst.

EISENRING: Ganz im Ernst.

SCHMITZ: Warum glauben Sie uns nicht?

EISENRING: Ihr Haus, Herr Biedermann, liegt sehr günstig, das müssen Sie einsehen: fünf solche Brandherde rings um die Gasometer, die leider bewacht sind, und dazu ein richtiger Föhn –

BIEDERMANN: Das ist nicht wahr.

SCHMITZ: Herr Biedermann! Wenn Sie uns schon für Brandstifter halten, warum nicht offen darüber reden?
Biedermann blickt wie ein geschlagener Hund.

BIEDERMANN: Ich halte Sie ja nicht für Brandstifter, meine Herren, das ist nicht wahr, Sie tun mir Unrecht, ich halte Sie nicht für – Brandstifter . . .

EISENRING: Hand aufs Herz!

BIEDERMANN: Nein! Nein, nein! Nein!

SCHMITZ: Aber wofür halten Sie uns denn?

BIEDERMANN: Für meine – Freunde . . .
Sie klopfen ihm auf die Schultern und lassen ihn stehen.
Wohin gehen Sie jetzt?

EISENRING: 's ist Zeit.

BIEDERMANN: Ich schwöre es Ihnen, meine Herren, bei Gott!

EISENRING: Bei Gott?

BIEDERMANN: Ja!
Er hält die Schwurfinger langsam hoch.*

SCHMITZ: Er glaubt nicht an Gott, der Willi, so wenig wie Sie, Herr Biedermann – da können Sie lange schwören.
Sie gehen weiter zur Türe.

BIEDERMANN: Was soll ich tun, daß Sie mir glauben?
Er vertritt ihnen den Ausgang.

EISENRING: Geben sie uns Streichhölzchen.

BIEDERMANN: Was – soll ich?

EISENRING: Wir haben keine mehr.

BIEDERMANN: Ich soll –

EISENRING: Ja, wenn Sie uns nicht für Brandstifter halten.

BIEDERMANN: Streichhölzchen?

SCHMITZ: Als Zeichen des Vertrauens, meint er.
Biedermann greift in seine Tasche.

EISENRING: Er zögert. Siehst du? Er zögert.

BIEDERMANN: Still! – aber nicht vor meiner Frau . . .
Babette kommt zurück.

BABETTE: Der Kaffee kommt sogleich.
Pause
Sie müssen gehen?

BIEDERMANN: Ja, meine Freunde – so schade es ist, aber – Hauptsache, daß Sie gespürt haben – Ich will nicht viel Worte machen,* meine Freunde, aber warum sagen wir einander eigentlich nicht du?

BABETTE: Hm.

BIEDERMANN: Ich bin dafür, daß wir Bruderschaft trinken!*
Er nimmt eine Flasche und den Korkenzieher.

EISENRING: Sagen Sie doch Ihrem lieben Mann, er soll deswegen keine Flasche mehr aufmachen, es lohnt sich nicht mehr.
Biedermann entkorkt.

BIEDERMANN: Es ist mir nichts zu viel, meine Freunde, nichts zu viel, und wenn Sie irgendeinen Wunsch haben – irgendeinen Wunsch . . . *Er füllt hastig die Gläser und gibt die Gläser.*
Meine Freunde, stoßen wir an!
Sie stoßen an.
Gottlieb. –
Er küßt Schmitz auf die Wange.

SCHMITZ: Sepp. –

BIEDERMANN: Gottlieb.
Er küßt Eisenring auf die Wange.

EISENRING: Willi. – *Sie stehen und trinken.*
Trotzdem, Gottlieb, müssen wir jetzt gehen.

SCHMITZ: Leider.

EISENRING: Madame –
Man hört Sirenen.

BABETTE: Es war ein reizender Abend.
Man hört Sturmglocken.

EISENRING: Nur noch eins, Gottlieb: –

BIEDERMANN: Was denn?

EISENRING: Du weißt es.

BIEDERMANN: Wenn Ihr irgendeinen Wunsch habt –

EISENRING: Die Streichhölzchen.
Anna ist eingetreten mit dem Kaffee.

BABETTE: Anna, was ist los?

ANNA: Der Kaffee.

BABETTE: Sie sind ja ganz verstört?

ANNA: Dahinten – der Himmel, Frau Biedermann, von der Küche aus – der Himmel brennt . . .
Es ist schon sehr rot, als Schmitz und Eisenring sich verneigen und gehen. Biedermann steht bleich und starr.

BIEDERMANN: Zum Glück ist's nicht bei uns . . . Zum Glück ist's nicht bei uns . . . Zum Glück –
Eintritt der Akademiker.

BIEDERMANN: Was wollen Sie?

DR. PHIL: Ich kann nicht länger schweigen.
Er nimmt ein Schriftstück aus der Brusttasche und verliest.
»Der Unterzeichnete, selber zutiefst erschüttert von den Ereignissen, die zur Zeit im Gang sind und die auch von unsrem Standpunkt aus, wie mir scheint, nur als verbrecherisch bezeichnet werden könne, gibt die folgende Erklärung zuhanden der Öffentlichkeit: – «
Viele Sirenen heulen, er verliest einen ausführlichen Text, wovon man aber kein Wort versteht, man hört

Hundegebell, Sturmglocken, Schreie, Sirenen in der Ferne, das Prasseln von Feuer in der Nähe; dann tritt er zu Biedermann und überreicht ihm das Schriftstück.
Ich distanziere mich –

BIEDERMANN: Und?

DR. PHIL: Ich habe gesagt, was ich zu sagen habe.
Er nimmt seine Brille ab und klappt sie zusammen.
Sehen Sie, Herr Biedermann, ich war ein Weltverbesserer, ein ernster und ehrlicher, ich habe alles gewußt, was sie auf dem Dachboden machten, alles, nur das eine nicht: Die machen es aus purer Lust!

BIEDERMANN: Herr Doktor –
Der Akademiker entfernt sich.
Sie, Herr Doktor, was soll ich damit?
Der Akademiker steigt über die Rampe und setzt sich ins Parkett.

BABETTE: Gottlieb –

BIEDERMANN: Weg ist er.

BABETTE: Was hast du denen gegeben? Ich hab's gesehen – Streichhölzer?

BIEDERMANN: Warum nicht.

BABETTE: Streichhölzer?

BIEDERMANN: Wenn die wirkliche Brandstifter wären, du meinst, die hätten keine Streichhölzer? . . . Babettchen, Babettchen!
Die Standuhr schlägt, Stille, das Licht wird rot, und man hört, während es dunkel wird auf der Bühne: Sturmglocken, Gebell von Hunden, Sirenen, Krach von stürzendem Gebälk, Hupen, Prasseln von Feuer, Schreie, bis der Chor vor die Szene tritt.

Chor
Sinnlos ist viel, und nichts
Sinnloser als diese Geschichte:
Die nämlich, einmal entfacht,*

Tötete viele, ach, aber nicht alle
Und änderte gar nichts.
Erste Detonation

CHORFÜHRER: Das war ein Gasometer.
Zweite Detonation

CHOR: Was nämlich jeder voraussieht
Lange genug,
Dennoch geschieht es am End:
Blödsinn,
Der nimmerzulöschende jetzt,
Schicksal genannt.*
Dritte Detonation

CHORFÜHRER: Noch ein Gasometer.
Es folgt eine Serie von Detonationen fürchterlicher Art.

CHOR: Weh uns! Weh uns! Weh uns!
Licht im Zuschauerraum.

NOTES TO THE TEXT

page

28 **Personen:** The names of the participants have been referred to as 'redende Namen', since they suggest the nature of their characters and could be seen to bring out their representative function.

'Bieder' originally suggested 'honest', but for over a century the word has been used (particularly in intellectual circles) to suggest bourgeois hypocrisy and narrow-mindedness. Frisch therefore invites us from the very start to see his central figure as a contemptible member of the middle class. His Christian name, 'Gottlieb' ('dear to God'), proves ironic in view of this character's actions and in terms of its contrast with his surname. More importantly, though, this surname suggests *representativeness*, which is conveyed by the generalising suffix ' -mann' and by the similarity of the whole word to 'Jedermann', the title of the internationally famous 'everyman' play by Hugo von Hofmannsthal. (If we miss this hint in the *dramatis personae*, the point is made overtly in Scene 6.) Another suggestion of a parallel with Hofmannsthal's play is evident in the name 'Knechtling'. If we remove the diminutive ending, we find 'Knecht': this not only suggests the character's role in Frisch's play, but it can be equated with Hofmannsthal's 'Schuld-

page

knecht', for whose miserable fate the central figure is likewise responsible. Such suggestions widen the relevance of the drama.

'Babette' (familiar form of Elisabeth) alliterates with 'Biedermann' and suggests immaturity; 'Anna' is equally pale (possibly reminiscent of the frightened young maid in Kafka's *Die Verwandlung*). The fire-raisers themselves also lack a sense of individuality: 'Schmitz' (= 'Smith'); 'Eisenring' (= 'ring of iron' - comically inappropriate to the physically weaker and more servile of the pair). There is no attempt to establish a sense of identity for either the policeman or the 'intellectual'.

Note Frisch's use of 'Mannen', a Swiss form of 'Männer'.

29 **des antiken Chors:** For details on the nature and function of the chorus, see the relevant section of the Introduction. Pupils may prefer to leave their reading of this scene, the most linguistically difficult of the play, until they have completed the rest. A simplified prose version is given below.

Note the way the clock chimes throughout this scene. An hour supposedly passes (and in the following scene Anna informs Biedermann that the man at the door arrived an hour earlier), and the scene closes on the stroke of nine. This hour is symbolic: Christ cried out, asking why he had been forsaken, 'at the ninth hour', and the nineteenth-century dramatist Friedrich Hebbel exploits this in his play *Maria Magdalene* in order to suggest a parallel between his heroine and Christ. Frisch's aims are less clear. He may be suggesting that God has now forsaken the world, and the society in which Biedermann lives is certainly one in which the absence of God or of belief is apparent. There are a number of blasphemous remarks in the rest of the play, and in the following scene Schmitz declares that people

page

do not believe in God any more – only in the fire service.
Bürger der Vaterstadt: The following contains a number of ambiguities but the general sense is that the vigilant can avoid disaster, a theme which the Chorus repeats throughout the play. The sense can better be grasped by recasting in prose: 'Bürger der Vaterstadt, seht uns. Wir sind Wächter der Vaterstadt, wir spähen, wir horchen, und wir sind freundlichgesinnt dem freundlichen Bürger – der uns ja schließlich bezahlt. Wir sind trefflich gerüstet, und wir wandeln um euer Haus, wachsam und arglos zugleich. Wir setzen uns manchmal, jedoch ohne zu schlafen, und wir spähen und horchen unermüdlich, damit sich enthüllt, was verhüllt und feuergefährlich ist, ehe es zu spät ist, das Feuer zu löschen. Vieles ist feuergefährlich, aber nicht alles, was feuert, ist unabwendbares Schicksal. Es gibt etwas, was auch Schicksal genannt wird (und man nennt es Schicksal, damit die Leute nicht fragen, wie es eigentlich kommt). Dies ist etwas Ungeheures, was Städte vernichten kann, aber es ist menschlicher, allzumenschlicher Unfug, der das sterbliche Bürgergeschlecht tilgt. Aber durch Vernunft kann man viel vermeiden. Wahrlich: Bloß weil etwas Blödsinniges geschehen ist, soll man es nicht "Schicksal" heißen. Gott verdient es nicht (daß die Menschen diese Art von Unfug begehen), und der Mensch, der Menschliches (menschlichen Unfug) so hoch achtet, verdient den Namen Mensch nicht, und er verdient die göttliche Erde nicht, die unerschöpflich ist und fruchtbar ist und dem Menschen gnädig ist, und er verdient die Luft nicht, die er atmet, und nicht die Sonne. Und der Blödsinn, der einst nicht zu löschen sein wird, verdient nicht, Schicksal zu heißen, bloß weil er geschehen ist.'

32 **Haarwasser:** 'hair tonic'; it soon transpires that Biedermann has made a fortune from his particular brand.

Note the way in which the reader's expectations are

page

defeated in Anna's following speech. We would imagine the pedlar wants money, food, or at least something tangible, but as in the rest of the play, it is the unexpected which repeatedly thwarts Biedermann. (We have already seen an example of Frisch's attempts to show characters talking at cross-purposes in Anna's protestation that she cannot throw the visitor out – we imagine humanitarian reasons forbid this act, but the reason lies rather in the visitor's physical strength.)

33 **Schmitz Josef:** Germans (and Swiss) often introduce themselves by placing the surname first.

Herr Biedermann brauchen: The (antiquated) use of the third-person plural here and elsewhere indicates respect for the person thus addressed.

Die Ringerei ist mir verleidet: German constructions of this sort are usually best translated by turning the indirect object into the subject of the English sentence: 'I've been put off/I'm sick of wrestling'. Note also the use of the suffix in 'Ringer*ei*' (instead of 'das Ringen'); 'ei' is often employed for pejorative force.

34 **Brot und Wein:** A rather obvious allusion to communion, and Schmitz seems to recognize the irony (although Biedermann possibly not – an early example of his general insensitivity). There would seem no deeper significance to this remark: no clear parallels can be drawn.

was Sie grad haben: (grad = gerade) 'Whatever you happen to have.' As Schmitz settles down, his language becomes more casual, and his elision of 'e' is frequent in verbs.

Stammtisch: a table reserved in a pub for a circle of friends who regularly meet there; it can also refer to the circle itself. Traditionally a place of honest talking.

35 **vom alten Schrot und Korn:** (usually 'vo*n* altem/echtem Schrot und Korn'), 'one of the old school', a wholly reliable type.

Das kommt davon: Here, and later in the scene, Schmitz

page

is being deliberately vague. Biedermann initially accepts this meaningless phrase, but when Schmitz repeats it, Biedermann effectively admits he did not understand the first usage by asking what does in fact produce the qualities in question.

Zivilcourage: 'The courage of one's convictions'. Schmitz uses a grandiose and inappropriate term, purely for the purposes of flattery.

der: The simple pronoun 'er' is appropriate here, but the relative pronoun is often used among the uneducated and in colloquial speech. This may be seen as part of an attempt to suggest Schmitz's lack of education.

Sie können mir. . .: The verb is suppressed, the listener being expected to supply an appropriately vulgar one. The sense is simply 'you can go to hell!'

36 **Gott hab ihn selig:** Usually 'habe', third person singular subjunctive to express a wish. ('May he rest in peace.')

es gibt sich, daß sie: 'they happen to. . .'

Köhler: 'Charcoal burner'. One of the many indirect (and also direct) references to fire in this scene. The ensuing pause may encourage us to speculate on this early influence in Schmitz's life.

ein großes Maul verreißt, weil er Schiß hat: 'Who talks big because he's (really) shit-scared.' As Schmitz becomes more confident, he relaxes control over the expressions he uses.

37 **unsereinen:** 'the likes of us'. (*Unsereiner* is declined like *dieser*, but used in the singular only.) Schmitz repeatedly makes reference to this idea.

schon hat er die Schulter gebrochen: 'And *I've* already broken *his* shoulder.' First Schmitz tries to win over the gullible Biedermann through ridiculous flattery, and now he is issuing indirect threats of violence.

39 **Es kommt ja doch . . . Gottesgericht:** As with his earlier use of 'das kommt davon', Schmitz is being deliberately vague at first. He then comes out with a pun on the word

page

'-gericht', which can mean either a 'court' or 'judgment' on the one hand, or a 'dish' or 'course' in a meal on the other. Biedermann has just insisted that one should know what is going to happen in the future, and Schmitz may therefore be suggesting that what awaits us is a judgment by God, or even, in the medieval sense of the word, a 'trial by ordeal'. However, since he has interrupted his thoughts by sniffing at the sausage, he may well have forgotten what he had in mind and mean 'this is a dish fit for the Gods'.

Weiß ich's?: 'How should I know?' Schmitz's flippant reply stands in marked contrast to Biedermann's horrified thought that the 'Gottesgericht' is indeed the judgment of God.

Ich habe Feierabend: 'I have finished my work for the day.' There is a clear difference between Biedermann's attitudes at work and those outside it. At work he is obviously ruthless and immoral; at home and in society he wishes to appear as generous and humane. This is clearly part of Frisch's attack on the ethics of the business world.

40 **Soll er. . .:** 'Just let him take on . . .' A threat, or challenge, is sometimes suggested by 'sollen', particularly when inversion takes place.

Vergelt's Gott: (S. German, Swiss and Austrian) 'Thank you.' The phrase is subjunctive ('may God reward you for it') and allows Schmitz another reference to the Almighty. In colloquial German this reference to God would pass unnoticed – the phrase is so common – but here we feel our attention is being drawn to the original sense. There is irony, therefore, in our suspicion that God will reward this 'kindness' in an inappropriate way. Schmitz uses the phrase on two further instances in the following scene.

41 **Sie entschuldigen:** The chorus has been sitting in the background, but we have almost forgotten its presence in

page

the course of this comic encounter. The 'illusion of reality' is now broken as both Biedermann and Schmitz speak directly to the firemen.

Spießer: (or 'Spießbürger') 'narrow-minded bourgeois', a well-known term of abuse. Both Biedermann and Babette are particularly anxious not to be seen as such, and this fear partly dictates their reactions to the fire-raisers.

Schaffell: Ingo Springmann points out a change from the *Hörspiel*, where a 'Ziegenfell' was referred to. The change may be seen to underline the image of Schmitz as a 'wolf in sheep's clothing'; he actually appears wearing this (white) sheepskin in the next scene.

42 **Schmitz muß lachen:** note a less common use of 'müssen' here – 'not to be able to help (doing something)'.

sie wendet sich an den Zuschauer: ('*die* Zuschauer' would be more common) another attempt to 'break' the theatrical 'illusion of reality'. Some of our amusement derives from the fact that this break is only partial: Babette still speaks as if she really were the wife of Biedermann!

seht/Wachen uns: 'seht uns wachen.'

zur Kurzweil: 'to entertain ourselves/pass the time.'

43 **. . . . Tilge die Vaterstadt uns:** 'daß ein Feuer unsere Vaterstadt nicht tilgt.'

Anruf genügt: 'a phone call will do'. Note once again the contrast between *what* the firemen say and *how* they say it, between the archaicisms of most of their speech, and the colloquialisms which deflate it, between the earnestness of their message, and the casual way in which their leader plays with his pipe.

Männer! . . . ein Schlafpulver: In her disgust, Babette omits several words, e.g. 'wenn sie nicht schlafen können . . .'

Strahl der Sonne: 'Der Tag, ein Strahl der Sonne, der aussieht wie eine Wimper des göttlichen Auges, leuchtet noch einmal über den traulichen Dächern der Stadt auf.'

page

45 **die Kehle schon umdrehn:** (coll.) 'I'll wring his neck before I'm finished with him!' The image underlines Biedermann's ruthlessness towards those who are helpless to oppose him.

er will gehen: Note the use of 'wollen' to indicate *intention* rather than desire. 'He is going to leave . . .'

47 **Tilsiter ist nämlich meine Leibspeis:** (= **Leibspeis*e***) Note that 'nämlich' does not have the sense of 'namely' here, but carries *explanatory* force (often translated as 'you know, you see').

There is considerable irony in this remark. Schmitz has used the same words with reference to the mustard, so we see another example of *repetition*, so common a feature of the characters' speeches (the fire-raisers later repeat a number of Biedermann's phrases). Because Schmitz has used the phrase before, he must have been lying on one occasion: another sign of his being prepared to do anything to achieve his ends. Schmitz's choice of the expensive cheese also reveals his aristocratic taste. Despite his supposedly impoverished youth, he has a finer palate than Biedermann and is even very fussy about the timing of his egg.

50 **drum geht die Welt in den Eimer:** (coll.) 'That's why the world's going to pot.' Note the way Schmitz plays on the middle class's horror of nationalisation ('Verstaatlichung'), a particular concern of the 1950s.

Metropol: suggests a high-class hotel or restaurant.

51 **der Ängstliche:** i.e. Biedermann. The chorus, as commonly in classical drama, treats the individual case in general terms. The syntax is here again complex. A 'prose' version would be the following: 'Der Ängstliche sieht viel, wo nichts eigentlich ist: Sein eigener Schatten schreckt ihn schon, er kämpft mit jedem Gerücht, und deshalb strauchelt er. Er lebt dahin, in diesem Zustand in dem man ihn so leicht erschrecken kann, bis es (das Böse) in seine Stube eintritt./Wie soll ich es deuten, daß diese

page

zwei das Haus nicht verlassen?/Der Ängstliche ist blinder als blind. Er zittert vor Hoffnung, daß es nicht das Böse sei, was kommt, und deshalb empfängt er es freundlich, ja wehrlos. Er ist müde durch die viele Angst und hofft immer auf das beste . . . bis es zu spät ist.

sind dabei: (coll.) 'are engaged in, are busy . . .' Frisch's stage directions are often casual, following the tone or mood of the play.

Gurren von Tauben: 'cooing of doves'. A discreet ironic touch repeated in Scene 4. The dove is traditionally symbolic of peace and tranquillity. (In the *Hörspiel* the doves are actually referred to as 'weiß', thus paralleling the white sheepskin and Eisenring's white waistcoat. A figure dressed completely in black appears later.)

Es poltert und rüttelt: German 'impersonal' constructions are often best translated by introducing a noun subject: 'The door is banged and shaken.'

53 **Wilhelm Maria Eisenring:** The second name is unusual (since it is feminine, sometimes adopted in honour of one's mother) and might possibly remind spectators of the second name of the famous aesthete and poet Rainer Maria Rilke. This would seem another ironic touch: Eisenring does have obvious aesthetic pretensions, which are seen most clearly in Scene 6.

Siehst du: 'I told you so.' Eisenring is trying to ingratiate himself with Biedermann by joining in the denunciation of Schmitz.

54 **Was ist das für eine Art:** ('Art' here has the sense of 'good behaviour, good manners') 'What sort of a way is that to behave?'

Was stellen Sie sich eigentlich vor: (coll.) 'Who do you think you are!'

Schließlich und endlich: (coll.) 'after all, when all's said and done.' The whole line is a splendid parody of Biedermann's own speech patterns.

55 **Was, zum Teufel, sollen diese Fässer hier?':** An infinitive might be expected after 'sollen', but this verb is

page

occasionally used without, the idea of 'purpose' being understood. 'What on earth/the devil are these drums doing here?' Note Biedermann's repeated reference to the devil – in contrast to Schmitz's regular references to God.

55 **Ja eben:** (coll.) 'Quite!' The phrase is often used without the 'ja' and expresses full agreement with the previous speaker. The last thing Biedermann expects is Eisenring to agree with him, but they are again talking at cross purposes. Eisenring is pretending to share Biedermann's anger and lay all the blame on Schmitz, who has miscalculated the number of drums that can easily be stored in the attic.

57 **Er fährt mit dem Finger über ein Faß:** (an unusual use of 'fahren' – to pass, slide over) 'He runs his finger over a barrel.'

Das kannst du einer Frau nicht zumuten: 'You can't expect that of a woman' – i.e. to put up with petrol in her loft. The fire-raisers again evade the issue by taking up one of the *possible*, rather than the central, aspects of Biedermann's attack.

58 **sich . . . unter den Gashahn gelegt:** 'put his head in the gas oven' (more commonly, 'den Gashahn aufdrehen').

unter vier Augen: 'in private'.

59 **Geht ja die Angestellten nichts an:** (note the colloquial omission of 'es' and the use of 'ja' as a mild intensifier) 'It's no concern of your staff, is it!'

HORMOFLOR: an ideal name for a hair tonic, combining the Greek *hormon* (from which we have 'hormone') and the Latin *florere* (to flourish).

Eine Seele von Mensch: (coll.) 'What a splendid fellow.'

60 **Strahl der Sonne:** Like everyone else in the play, the chorus repeats itself. The line lengths are here slightly different from those in Scene 1, but the effect of this free verse is much the same.

Der, um zu wissen: The following speech should be seen as a contrast to 'Klug ist . . . der Mensch . . . wenn er

page

bedenkt, was er sieht'. Instead of reflecting on what he can actually *see*, man will instead read newspapers, become incensed over things which take place miles away, rest content with other people's interpretations, and read only about what happened the day before. He will not see through the obvious and outrageous things happening within his own house, which are as yet unpublished.

61 **schwenkt die Front:** 'wheels round' (in military fashion) – in order to stop Biedermann's progress.

62 **ja:** here used as an emotive particle, suggesting the speaker expects his request to be fulfilled. 'Let me through, will you!'

Der nämlich zusieht: ('nämlich' here has explanatory force) 'Der Chor, der nämlich von außen zusieht, kann leichter begreifen, was droht.'

kalten Schweißes gefaßt: 'composed, but in a cold sweat'. Typical of the curious mixture of emotions revealed by the chorus.

ich bin eilig: (coll.) usually 'ich habe es eilig'.

Heilig sei Heiliges uns: The chorus is here making fun of the view that property is sacred. 'Was heilig ist, soll uns heilig bleiben, nämlich das Eigentum. Was auch aus diesem Eigentum entstehen sollte – auch wenn es einst etwas ist, was man nicht löschen kann und uns dann alle versengt und verkohlt – trotzdem soll das was heilig ist, auch uns heilig bleiben.'

64 **Schien es ihm denkbar?:** 'schien es ihm denkbar, daß die zwei Männer seine Güte mißbrauchen würden?'

65 **Ängstlich-verwegen:** The paradox is probably best brought out by inserting a conjunction: 'timid yet daring'.

Der die Verwandlungen scheut: 'he who fears changing', i.e. who is more afraid of changing himself and his attitudes than he is of facing disaster.

66 **Lili Marlen:** A German song, particularly popular among soldiers during the Second World War. The version sung

page

every night by Lale Andersen on 'Radio Belgrade' captured the imagination of Allied soldiers too, thus ensuring international popularity. In the *Hörspiel* Eisenring whistles tunes from Strauss's light-hearted *Der Rosenkavalier*, the libretto of which was written by Hofmannsthal. The tune is thus an ironic way of recalling the author of *Jedermann*. Frisch's decision to change to 'Lili Marlen' suggests a desire to recall the Third Reich, one of the possible models of application of his 'parable'.

den Zeigfinger: usually 'Zeig*e*finger', index finger.

Was hast du davon!: (coll.) 'What good will that do you/us?'

67 **Föhn:** a warm, dry wind, particularly to the north and south of the Alps.

68 **Benutzen Sie getrost mein Badzimmer:** (usually 'Bad*e*zimmer') 'Do feel free to use my bathroom.'

was können wir dafür: (coll.) 'it's not our fault that . . .'

69 **daß ich keinen Humor habe:** 'that I have no sense of humour'. Biedermann again shows himself anxious not to be considered a 'Spießbürger'.

die schwarze Witwe Knechtling: It is difficult to see Frisch's aim in introducing this (non-speaking) character. Biedermann dismisses her heartlessly at the beginning of Scene 5, and that may reveal another sign of his lack of remorse, even at this stage. A more important function may be evident only in performance. The widow will, in Swiss custom, be dressed entirely in black (including black veil): she may appear to the spectator, therefore, as another figure of 'death'. She will be sitting in the living room throughout the next scene, which takes place 'above' and in which preparations for destruction are being made. Both 'above' and 'below', then, Biedermann is threatened by symbols of death.

Holzwolle ist doch keine Sache: (coll.) 'Wood shavings shouldn't be a problem.'

70 **Gleichmacherei:** (pejorative) 'making everyone equal'.

page

72 **Sodom und Gomorra:** According to the Old Testament, the towns of Sodom and Gomorrah were destroyed *by fire* because of the wickedness of their inhabitants. The idea here seems to be that the notion of 'human goodness' is as repulsive to Biedermann's friends as were Sodom and Gomorrah to the Almighty.

seien Sie getrost: Eisenring is reassuring Biedermann that his bourgeois friends (who supposedly lack Biedermann's fine sense of humour) will be just as helpless as him when disaster finally strikes.

Wenn das kein Polizeistaat ist: Eisenring expects the hearer to provide the logical conclusion to his remark: 'If this isn't a police state, then what is!'

74 **so ernst, bis es reicht zum Verrat:** 'so serious that it reaches the point of treason'. An ironic remark, since accusations of treason are usually made only by those who abide by the law. Frisch here goes out of his way to emphasize the wholly non-ideological stance of the fire-raisers.

75 **Kirchenglockengeläute:** These bells become particularly loud at the beginning of Scene 5. Bells have traditionally served a double role: to call the believers for worship; and to warn of impending danger. Biedermann ignores their message, even when they become louder still. In Scene 5 he (symbolically) has the windows closed to exclude the urgent warning.

dann ist unser Haarwasser hin: (coll.) 'then that'll be the end of our hair tonic'.

kaum war er in der Partei: 'hardly had he joined the party, when . . .'. Any reference to 'the Party' in the 1950s inevitably meant Hitler's National Socialist Party. Babette's suggestion is that her husband has not derived full benefit from his actions, whether in becoming a Nazi or marketing his hair tonic. Like the reference to 'Lili Marlen', this allusion encourages the spectator to see (partial) parallels in the Third Reich.

page

es heiligt die Mittel . . . der Zweck: 'Der Zweck heiligt die Mittel' – 'the end justifies the means', a proverb popular with extremist politicians.

bieder-unbieder: 'honestly-dishonest', 'honest yet dishonest', i.e. he is dishonest in that he breaks the law, but he is honest in that he does so for the sake of a higher ideal. Some critics have suggested that by using these particular adjectives in this paradox, the chorus puts the Dr. phil. on a par with the central character. Like *Bieder*mann, he may be anxious to deceive himself concerning the true nature of the fire-raisers – until, of course, it is too late.

78 **wie beim Abendmahl:** 'as at communion'. 'Abendmahl' suggests both 'communion', and, of course, Christ's 'Last Supper'. Within half a page, therefore, there are two suggestions that Biedermann is about to die. The idea of a 'grand meal' may remind the spectator of the meal that Hofmannsthal's Jedermann throws for his guests – in the middle of which the figure of 'death' appears.

79 **Bitte sehr:** 'There you are!' An ironic response to Biedermann's last request.

mit einer Rose: In polite German society it is considered appropriate to bring a small token of appreciation when arriving for a dinner party. The guests are revealed as conforming to the etiquette of the middle class, all the other trappings of which Biedermann has just cast aside.

80 **im vollen Gang:** (usually 'in vollem Gang') 'in full swing'.

81 **Was macht denn die Holzwolle?:** (coll.) 'How are you getting on with your wood shavings?'

was ist der Witz dran?: (coll.) 'What's so funny about it?'

andere Kreise, andere Witze!: A variation of the well-known proverb, 'andere Länder, andere Sitten', 'other people have different ways of doing things'. Probably

page

best translated here by something like 'different jobs, different jokes'.

den man ins Bockshorn jagen kann: (coll.) 'who can be scared out of his wits'. The context suggests the force of the verb is fairly strong here, although it can have the milder sense of 'bully', 'browbeat', 'intimidate'. There is also another sense of the verb, namely, to 'fool', 'lead up the garden path'. Compare the senses of 'verkohlen', used earlier in the play and especially in the 'Burleske'.

82 **Ihre Gans, Madame, ist Klasse:** 'Your goose, my dear lady, is fantastic.' A humorous combination of the formal ('Madame') and the colloquial ('Klasse').

The choice of a goose may be an echo of Brecht's *Leben des Galilei* (in the final scene of which the hero feeds gluttonously on the same bird). Hans Bänziger has suggested further parallels between these scenes, but these are just as likely to be coincidences. For further details, see his *Zwischen Protest und Traditionsbewußtsein*, p. 61 and p. 115.

Pommard: One of Burgundy's fine (and expensive) red wines.

Es muß aber nicht sein!: Note the force of 'müssen' with 'nicht': 'there's no *need* for it/it's not essential'.

83 **so sind halt die Leute aus dem Volk:** 'halt' is used widely in the South in the sense of 'eben'. Here it carries explanatory force: 'that's just the way the common people tend to be'.

84 **Ich kann doch nichts dafür!:** (coll.) 'It's not my fault!'

Das ist es: (coll.) 'That's the problem.' In the final lines of this speech Eisenring seems to be suggesting a motive for his actions: psychological trauma (through a deprived childhood) has produced his envy of the rich. However, this motif is not developed elsewhere.

85 **Cave de l'Echannon:** This would seem to be an invention. 1949 was, however, a very good year for burgundy.

page

86 **Haben sie Kandelaber . . .:** The inversion conveys a sense of surprise: 'They've got candlesticks and yet they hide them!'

87 **und wenn er's mir hundertmal sagt:** 'even if he were to tell me a hundred times/however many times he told me.'

88 **Dabei ist er begabt:** A less common use of 'dabei' in the sense of 'and yet, despite this'.

JEDERMANN!: Schmitz (again dressed ironically in white) is not playing the part of a ghost, but the figure of 'Tod' in Hofmannsthal's *Jedermann* (see also the relevant section of the Introduction). In that play Jedermann (who is based on the medieval 'Everyman' figure) heeds the warning of 'Death' and is finally saved. As Babette goes on to suggest, she and her husband have both seen the play in its most famous production: that at Salzburg. They have, however, learnt nothing from it. Babette vaguely remembers the scene in question; her husband has forgotten it completely. The suggestions of this 'play within the play' are that what Biedermann has failed to heed on one occasion, he is unlikely to heed on a second.

89 **Sonst wird er seinen Text nicht los:** (coll.) 'Otherwise he won't be able to get through his lines.'

der Geist von Hamlet: Biedermann here displays gross cultural ignorance. He dismisses the sound suggestion made by his wife and proposes instead a number of figures who are in some way connected with the theme of vengeance. The ghost in *Hamlet*, for example, is Hamlet's father, who urges his son to avenge him. The 'Stone Guest' in the Don Juan legend avenges the seduction of his daughter; and the ghost in *Macbeth*, far from being Macbeth's 'assistant', is that of the dead Banquo (whom Macbeth has had murdered), who attempts to stop Macbeth taking the King's seat at dinner.

90 **aber zum Hinstellen . . .:** Eisenring affects mock horror,

page

suppressing the final part of his accusation: 'but that you should go and portray him. . .'. Through the details he employs to accuse Schmitz of insensitivity, Eisenring reveals not only his own insensitivity, but also the ability to play forcefully on the conscience of Biedermann. The latter is shaken, but unlike Jedermann, he is unrepentant.

91 **Fuchs, du hast die Gans gestohlen:** This (children's) song arises seemingly naturally (as Schmitz tries to extricate himself from an embarrassing situation), but it has obvious thematic significance. Biedermann may be seen to represent the fox, and the arsonists the hunter. The goose could refer to Knechtling's invention or possibly, as one critic has suggested, to Biedermann's material possessions in general. At any rate, these lines again raise the theme of vengeance.

In the *Hörspiel*, the song is introduced in a more clearly symbolic role. Biedermann confesses that he has 'done wrong' in his life, and Schmitz trivializes this by asking whether he has stolen the goose. Biedermann's reply ('Das gerade nicht – ') suggests that his own crime can at least be compared with such a theft.

Scheißgewehr: a standard pun on *schießen/scheißen* – to shoot/shit. Biedermann again attempts to show his scorn for middle-class notions of propriety by pretending to find the pun amusing.

92 **was:** colloquial for 'warum'.

93 **die Schwurfinger:** i.e. thumb, index and second fingers.

94 **Ich will nicht viel Worte machen:** 'I don't want to go on at great length'/'to put it briefly'. Note the use of 'viel' in this set phrase; 'viel*e*', expected grammatically, is also used.

Bruderschaft trinken: (usually 'Br*ü*derschaft') Brief ceremony of mutual toasts, handshakes, kisses or the like, after which one addresses the other as 'du'. Probably best translated as 'let's drink to our friendship'.

96 **einmal entfacht:** 'once it has been set ablaze'.

page

97 **Schicksal genannt:** 'Was jedermann lange genug vorausgesehen hat, geschieht am Ende: Wir können dieses Feuer jetzt nie löschen, es ist durch nichts als Blödsinn geschehen, aber alle nennen es einfach "Schicksal" '. The key words 'Blödsinn' and 'Schicksal', previously raised by the chorus, are again brought together.

SELECT VOCABULARY

The following list omits the 'Grundwortschatz' and gives the meaning of words for their context in the play alone. (If used in different contexts, meaning is supplied in order of occurrence.) In general, words covered in the notes are not repeated here.

Weak masculine nouns are indicated as follows: **der Mensch, en, en**; adjectival nouns: **der Freundlichgesinnt–**; separable verbs: **an·gehen**; strong verbs: **braten, ie, a** (= **briet, gebraten**); plurals of nouns are also indicated in the traditional manner.

das Abendmahl (no pl.) Holy Communion
ab·machen settle, agree; **abgemacht** 'agreed!', 'done!'
abgesehen von irrespective of, apart from
ab·stellen to put down
ab·wischen to wipe off
achten to respect
der Akademiker, – person with a university education
alle: sie sind alle they are finished
allerschwerst- most serious, difficult of all
alleweil always, all the time
allzumenschlich all-too-human
das Allzuverdächtige that which is all too suspicious
altmodisch old-fashioned
an·bieten, o, o to offer
an·blicken to look at
an·gehen, i, a to concern
an·heben, o,o start, begin
an·knipsen switch on

der **Anruf, -e** telephone call
die **Anschrift, -en** inscription
an·starren to stare at
an·stoßen, ie, o toast, clink glasses
antik ancient
der **Anwalt, ¨-e** lawyer
an·weisen, ie, ie show, direct towards
an·zeigen to report (to the police)
an·zünden to light up
arglos innocent; guileless
der **Argwohn** (no pl.) suspicion
der **Ärmel, -** sleeve
der **Aschenbecher, -** ashtray
auf·atmen to breathe a sigh of relief
auf·drängen to intrude, impose oneself
auf·gehen, i, a to open (intrans.)
auf·hängen, i, a hang, string up
auf·heben, o, o to lift up
auf·leuchten to light up, shine
aufmerkend attentive, alert
die **Aufregung** (no pl.) excitement
auf·reißen, i, i to rip open
aufrichtig sincere
auf·schlagen, u, a to open
auf·treiben, ie, ie to get hold of
augenblicklich immediately
aus·blasen, ie, a to blow out
aus·brechen, a, o to break out
ausdrücklich expressly
der **Ausgang** (no pl. in this sense) time off (after work)
ausgenommen except
ausgerechnet of all things/people
ausgesprochen marked, pronounced
aus·halten to bear, put up with
aus·löffeln to spoon out (until empty)
aus·machen to constitute, amount to; **es macht nichts aus** it doesn't matter; **wenn es nichts ausmacht** if it's all the same to you
aus·nutzen to exploit
das **Außenviertel, -** outlying district
die **Äußerlichkeit, en** outward appearance

die **Barmherzigkeit** (no pl.) compassion, mercy
bedenken, a, a to think about, contemplate
die **Bedingung, en** condition
sich **befassen (mit)** to concern oneself (with)
befestigen to fasten
begabt talented
begraben, u, a to bury
begreifen, i, i to understand
behandeln to treat
sich **beherrschen** to control oneself
bekanntlich as is well known

sich **beklagen** to complain
bekümmern to trouble, upset
belesen well read
belustigen to amuse
das **Benzin** (no pl.) petrol
der **Benzingeruch** (no pl.) smell of petrol
bereuen to regret
sich **beruhigen** to calm down
beschlagnahmen to impound, confiscate
die **Besprechung, en** conference, discussion
das **Besteck, e** cutlery
bestellen to order
die **Bestie, n** beast
sich **betätigen** to busy oneself
die **Beteiligung** (no pl.) participation, share
bevorstehen, a, a (with dat.) to be in store (for someone)
bewachen to guard
die **Bildung** (no pl.) education
bitterernst deadly serious
blank: die blanke Wahrheit the naked truth
blasen, ie, a to blow
das **Blech** (no pl.) metal
der **Blödsinn** (no pl.) folly, stupidity
der **Brandherd, e** heart of a fire
der **Brandstifter, -** arsonist
die **Brandstifterei** (no pl.) arson
die **Brandstiftung** (no pl.) arson
braten, ie, a to roast
der **Brennstoff, e** inflammable matter, fuel
der **Brillenträger, -** man wearing glasses
sich **bücken** to bow
die **Bühne, n** the stage
der **Bürger, -** citizen
das **Bürgergeschlecht** race of citizens
das **Burgunderglas, ¨er** glass of burgundy (wine)
der **Bursche, n, n** fellow

der **Chor, -e** chorus
der **Chorführer, -** leader of the chorus

dabei and yet; as well, into the bargain
der **Dachboden, ¨** attic
die **Dachrinne, n** gutter
dahinleben to go on living
der **Damast** (no pl.) damask
der **Dämmerdunkel** (no pl.) half-light
der **Dank** (no pl.) thanks
darum for that reason; that's why
der **Defaitismus** (no pl.) defeatism
die **Detonation, en** detonation
deuten to interpret, explain
die **Deutung, en** interpretation
das **Dienstmädchen, -** maid

der Dingsda (coll.) what's-his-name
sich distanzieren to dissociate oneself
der Doktor, en doctor
Dr. phil. = Ph.D. (Doctor of Philosophy)
dran = daran; was ist der Witz dran what's the joke?
drauf = darauf; drauf und dran sein to be just about to
sich drehen to turn oneself round
dringend urgent
drohen to threaten
dröhnend roaring, booming
der Druck, ¨e pressure
drücken to press
drum = darum for that reason, that's why
der Duft, ¨e fragrance, smell
duften to smell
dulden to tolerate, put up with
dünken to seem
durch·führen to carry out
durch·schauen to see through
duschen to have a shower

eben precisely; just now
ebensogut just as well
das Ehrenwort (no pl.) word of honour
eigenhändig with one's own hands
das Eigentum (no pl.) property
der Eimer, - pail; **in den Eimer gehen** go down the drain, go to the dogs
eindeutig plain, clear
der Eindruck, ¨e impression
ein·gehen, i, a to agree, fall in with
das Einkommen (no pl.) income
ein·nehmen: eine Stellung einnehmen to take up a position
sich einnisten to settle in
die Einstellung, en attitude
das Einzigrichtige the only right thing
die Eisblume, n 'frost-flowers' (as created on glass, table-cloths, etc.)
entfachen kindle
enthüllen to reveal
entkorken to uncork
entlassen, ie, a dismiss, sack
entrüstet angry, provoked
das Ereignis, sse event
die Erfindung, en invention
der Erfinder, - inventor
erfreuen: sehr erfreut pleased to meet you
sich erheben, o, o to get up
sich erholen to recover
die Erklärung, en explanation
der Ernst (no pl.) seriousness; **im Ernst** seriously
erschöpfen exhaust
erschrecken, a, o to be startled
erschüttern to shock
erstaunlicherweise astonishingly

der **Estrich, e** attic
das **Etablissement, s** establishment
die **Etikette, n** label

das **Faß, ¨sser** barrel
sich **fassen** to compose oneself; **sich kurz fassen** to be brief
die **Faust, ¨e** fist
fehlen to be lacking
fertig werden, u, o to cope with
feuergefährlich (highly) inflammable
das **Feuergefährliche** the (highly) inflammable
feuern to burn
die **Feuersbrunst, ¨e** fire, conflagration
die **Feuerversicherung, en** fire insurance
die **Feuerwehr** fire brigade
feuerwehrgleich like the fire brigade
der **Feuerwehrmann, ¨er** fireman
finden: was finden Sie dazu? what do you think of that?
finster dark
flink brisk
der **Flur, e** hall
foppen to fool, pull someone's leg
fort·schicken to send away
der **Frack, s** or **¨e** tail coat, tails
die **Frage: in Frage kommen** to come into question
frei: ich bin so frei may I?
freilich of course
der **Freundlichgesinnt-** the well-disposed person
fruchtbar fruitful
der **Funke, n** (gen. **ns**) spark
futtern (coll.) tuck in, eat heartily

die **Gattin, nen** wife
das **Gebälk** (no pl.) timbers, timberwork
das **Gebell** (no pl.) barking
gefallen: sich (dat.) **etwas gefallen lassen** to put up with something
der **Gefängniswagen, -** police van
das **Geflügelmesser, -** poultry knife
das **Gegenteil, e** opposite; **im Gegenteil** on the contrary
gehören to belong
der **Geist, er** ghost
das **Gekreisch** (no pl.) shrieking
das **Gelächter** (no pl.) laughter
das **Geläute** (no pl.) ringing of bells
gemütlich cosy
genaugenommen strictly speaking
die **Genehmigung** (no pl.) approval, licence
genußvoll full of pleasure, with obvious enjoyment
das **Gepolter** (no pl.) racket, din
der **Geruch, ¨e** smell
das **Gerücht, e** rumour

gerüstet equipped
geschäftlich on a business matter
das **Geschöpf, e** creature
geschult schooled, trained
geschwind rapidly
der **Geselle, n, n** fellow
die **Gesellschaft, en** company
gesinnt disposed towards
gestatten to allow, permit
das **Getue** (no pl.; coll.) fuss, goings on
der **Gewohnheitskuß, ⸚e** usual, perfunctory kiss
gewohnt: es gewohnt sein to be used to (something)
geziemen befit, become
das **Gitterfenster, -** barred window
die **Glatze, n** bald head
gnädig merciful
göttlich divine
grölen to bawl
großartig wonderful, splendid
günstig favourable
die **Gurke, n** gherkin
gurren to coo
die **Güte** (no pl.) kindness
die **Gutmütigkeit** (no pl.) kindheartedness

halt (emotive particle) simply, just
halten, ie, a: halten für to take to be
der **Halunke, n** (gen. ns) scoundrel
handeln: sich handeln um to concern, be about
das **Handgelenk, e** wrist
die **Handschellen** (pl.) handcuffs
das **Hanebüchene** (no pl.) the outrageous, preposterous
hantieren to fiddle around
der **Harn** (no pl.) urine
der **Haspel, -** reel
das **Häubchen, -** bonnet
sich hauen to beat, strike oneself
der **Hauseigentümer, -** house owner
der **Hausierer, -** pedlar
heben, o, o to lift
der **Helm, e** helmet
Herrgottnochmal! for God's sake!
herumfingern: an seinen Fingern herumfingern to fiddle with one's fingers
das **Heulen** (no pl.) howling, screaming
hinaus·schmeißen, i, i to throw, chuck out
hintenherum behind one's back
die **Holzwolle** (no pl.) wood wool
horchen to listen
der **Humor: keinen Humor haben** to have no sense of humour
das **Hundegebell** (no pl.) barking of dogs
das **Hupen** (no pl.) tooting of a horn
husten to cough
der **Hydrant, en, en** hydrant
ideologisch ideological

sich irren to be mistaken

der **Jäger, -** hunter
jemals ever
der **Jurist, en, en** lawyer

kampfmutig courageous in battle
der **Kandelaber, -** candelabra
die **Kastanie, n** chestnut
kaufmännisch commercial
die **Kehle, n** throat
kennerhaft like an expert
der **Klassenunterschied, e** class difference
knallrot bright red
die **Knallzündschnur, ¨e** detonating fuse
der **Köhler, -** charcoal burner
die **Köhlerhütte, n** charcoal burner's hut
der **Korkenzieher, -** corkscrew
kosten taste, savour
kränken to hurt, insult
der **Kranz, ¨e** wreath
kristallen crystal
krumm: etwas krumm nehmen to take something amiss
der **Kübel, -** bucket
die **Kündigung** (no pl.) notice of dismissal
kurz: kurz und gut in short

lassen: in Ruhe lassen to leave in peace
die **Lederbinde, n** leather strap
die **Ledermappe, n** leather briefcase
die **Lehre, n** lesson, moral
das **Lehrstück, e** didactic play, morality play
die **Leibspeise, n** favourite dish
sich **etwas leisten** to afford something
die **Leistung, en** achievement
lichterloh blazing
lohnen: es lohnt sich nicht mehr there's no point, it's not worth it
löschen to extinguish
lösen to loosen
die **Lösung, en** solution
die **Lukarne, n** attic window
lustig merry, gay

machen: es macht mir nichts it doesn't bother me
die **Männerwelt** (no pl.) the world of men
die **Mark: durch Mark und Bein gehen** cut to the quick
die **Marmelade** (no pl.) jam
das **Maß: alles mit Maß** everything in moderation
das **Maul, ¨er** mouth (of animals; vulg. of persons)
mehrstimmig as arranged for several voices
menschlich human
die **Menschlichkeit** (no pl.) humaneness, humanity
messen, a, e to measure
das **Messerbänklein** cutlery rest
das **Messing** brass
mißbrauchen abuse
das **Mißtrauen** mistrust

der **Mitarbeiter, -** assistant
mitbürgerlich in communal spirit
der **Mittelstand** middle class
das **Muster, -** pattern
mustern examine, survey

nagen to gnaw
sich **nähen** to approach
nämlich actually, you see; namely
nässen to wet
neidlos without envy
nervenzerrüttet with shattered nerves
neuerdings again
nimmer never
nimmermehr nevermore
das **Nimmerzulöschende** what cannot be extinguished
das **Notizbüchlein, -** small notebook

obdachlos homeless
der **Obdachlos-** homeless person
offengesprochen speaking frankly
das **Offenkundige** the obvious
die **Öffentlichkeit** the public
ohnmächtig helpless

packen seize, take hold of
das **Parkett** 'stalls' of a theatre
passen to suit
die **Peitsche, n** whip
die **Pfanne, n** pan
die **Platte, n** tray; dish
der **Plunder** (no pl.) junk, rubbish
die **Polterei** (no pl.) racket, din
poltern to rattle, bang
prasseln to crackle
die **Probe, n** rehearsal
prost! cheers!
die **Protzerei** (no pl.) showing off
der **Prozeß, sse** lawsuit
prüfen to test, examine
die **Putzfäden** (pl.) cotton waste

der **Quadratmeter, -** square metre
der **Quatsch** (coll., no pl.) rubbish

die **Rasierklinge, n** razor blade
die **Rechnung, en** bill
regelrecht regular
reglos motionless
riechen, o, o to smell; to smell of
ringen, a, u to wrestle
der **Ringer, -** wrestler
ringsum round about
das **Rotkraut,** (no pl.) red cabbage
rücksichtslos ruthless
rundheraus bluntly, plainly
rüsten to prepare

der **Sachverständig-** expert
sage und schreibe believe it or not
satt: es satt haben (coll.) to be fed up with something
saufen, o, o to drink (of animals, vulg. of persons)

das **Schaffel, –e** sheepskin
der **Schenkel, –** thigh
scherzen to joke
scheuen to shun
das **Schicksal, e** fate
das **Schlafpulver, –** sleeping powder
der **Schlag, ¨e** stroke
der **Schlauch, ¨e** hose
schleichen, i, i to creep, sneak out
die **Schleife, n** bow
schleudern to hurl
schmatzen to munch loudly
schnappen to catch, 'nab'
schnarchen to snore
schnuppern to sniff
die **Schnur, ¨e** fuse, flex
der **Schöpfer, –** creator
schrauben to screw
schreckhaft easily frightened
das **Schriftstück, e** document
das **Schürzchen, –** small apron
schwatzen to gossip
die **Schwelle, n** threshold
schwergewicht heavy-weight
seinerseits for his part
der **Senf** (no pl.) mustard
servieren to serve (a meal)
sichtlich obviously
der **Silberkübel, –** silver bucket (for cooling wine)
sinnlos senseless, pointless
sorgsam careful
spähen to watch, be on the lookout for
der **Spaß, ¨e** joke; **Spaß beiseite** joking apart
die **Spaßigkeit** (no pl., Swiss) merriment
der **Spießer, –** narrow-minded individual
spüren to feel, perceive
das **Städtevernichtende** that which destroys cities
der **Stadtteil, e** district of a city
der **Standpunkt, e** point of view
die **Standuhr, en** grandfather clock
stapeln to stack up
starr rigid
steif stiff
steinern made of stone
die **Stellung, en** position, attitude
sterblich mortal
stier vacant, blank
stiften to donate
die **Stimmung** (no pl.) mood, atmosphere
stopfen to fill (a pipe)
stören to disturb
die **Strafanstalt, en** prison
strafbar punishable
der **Strahl, e** ray, beam
straucheln to stumble, fall
das **Streichholz, ¨er** match
strömen to pour, stream
die **Stube, n** room, living room
der **Stundenschlag** (no pl.) striking of the hour

das Tablettchen, - small tray
die Tafel, n table (laid out for meal)
die Tarnung, en camouflage
die Tätowierung (no pl.) tattoo
das Tatsächliche (no pl.) the real
die Taube, n pigeon, dove
tauchen to dip
die Theatersprache (no pl.) language of the theatre
tilgen to eradicate
tönen to sound
das Traktat, e tract, pamphlet
das Trauma, -ta psychological trauma
das Treppenhaus, ¨-er stairwell
der Tüchtig- capable, competent person
die Turmuhr, en church clock

überhaupt at all
überreichen to hand over
üblich usual
sich um·drehen to turn around
der Umstand, ¨-e circumstances; **keine Umstände!** don't go to any trouble!
unabwendbar unavoidable
unerschöpflich inexhaustible
der Unfug (no pl.) nonsense, mischief
die Ungeduld (no pl.) impatience
das Ungeheure (no pl.) a monstrous thing
unglaublich unbelievable
das Unheil disaster
der Unmensch, en, en inhuman person
der Unselig- unfortunate, wretched person
der Unsinn (no pl.) nonsense
unterbrechen, a, o to interrupt
der Untersuchungsrichter, - examining magistrate
der Unterzeichnet- undersigned
der Untüchtig- incapable, incompetent person
unvergeßlich unforgettable
das Unveröffentlichte (no pl.) that which is unpublished
die Unverschämtheit (no pl.) outrageous, impertinent act; insolence

verängstigt frightened
verbergen, a, o to hide
sich verbitten, a, e to refuse to put up with
die Verblüffung (no pl.) amazement
verbrecherisch criminal
die Verbrüderung (no pl.) fraternisation
der Verdacht (no pl.) suspicion
verdammtnochmal! damn and blast, bloody hell!
sich vergewissern to make sure
verhaften to arrest
das Verhör, e hearing, trial
das Verhüllte (no pl.) that

which is covered, concealed
verkehrt wrong
verkohlen to become charred
verlassen: sich verlassen auf to rely on
die **Verlegenheit** (no pl.) embarrassment
verlesen, a, e to read out
vermeiden, ie, ie to avoid
vernehmen, a, o to perceive
sich **verneigen** to bow
die **Vernunft** (no pl.) reason, intelligence
verpfuscht bungled
sich **verrechnen** to miscalculate
verriegelt bolted, locked
verrostet rusty
verrückt: zum Verrückt-werden enough to drive you mad
sich **versammeln** to gather together
die **Versicherung, en** insurance company
versperren to block, obstruct
die **Verstaatlichung** (no pl.) nationalisation
verstecken to hide
verstört troubled, distraught
vertreten, a, e to block, bar
die **Verwandlung, en** transformation, metamorphosis
verwechseln confuse, mix up
verwirren to confuse, bewilder
sich **verziehen, o, o** to withdraw
die **Visitenkarte, n** visiting card
der **Völkerstamm, ⸚e** race of people
voran·gehen, i, a to go ahead, take the lead
voraus·sehen, a, e to foresee
vorbei·sausen to whistle by
vorkommen, a, o to happen
die **Vorschrift, en** rule, regulation
die **Vorsichtsmaßnahme, n** precautionary measure
vor·treten to step forward

die **Wache, n** watch
wachsam watchful, vigilant
der **Wächter** guardian, watchman
wahrlich, truly, 'verily'
das **Waisenhaus, ⸚er** orphanage
wandeln to walk
die **Wange, n** cheek
die **Wasserschale, n** finger bowl
der **Wechselgesang** (no pl.) singing in alternate parts
wehrlos defenceless, helpless
die **Weitsicht** (no pl.) far-sightedness

der **Weltverbesserer, -** world reformer, idealist
sich **wenden (an),** make application to, consult
die **Weste, n** waistcoat
widerlich disgusting
die **Wimper, n** eyelash
die **Wirtschaft, en** pub; customers in a pub
die **Witwe, n** widow
wohnhaft resident at

das **Zeichen, -** sign
zeitig in good time
das **Zeughaus, ¨er** arsenal
sich **zieren** to need a lot of pressing, refuse out of politeness
zittern to tremble
zögern hesitate
zu·greifen, i, i to help oneself
zuhanden into the hands of
zu·muten to expect (of someone)
die **Zündkapsel, n** detonator
die **Zündschnur, ¨e** fuse
zusammen·falten to fold up
zusammen·klappen to fold together
zu·schauen to watch
der **Zustand, ¨e** condition
zutiefst deeply, profoundly
der **Zweck, e** purpose; **es hat keinen Zweck** it's no use